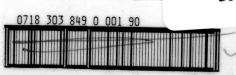

POOR BLOODY INFANTRY

A Memoir of the
First World War

W.H.A. Groom

WILLIAM KIMBER · LONDON

First published in 1976 by
WILLIAM KIMBER & CO. LIMITED
Godolphin House, 22a Queen Anne's Gate,
London, SW1H 9AE

© W.H.A. Groom, 1976
ISBN 0 7183 0384 9 ✓

Filmset by
Specialised Offset Services Ltd., Liverpool
and printed in Great Britain by
The Pitman Press, Bath

POOR BLOODY INFANTRY

*FOR THE GRANDCHILDREN
OF MY GENERATION.*

Contents

List of Illustrations

*All photographs are reproduced by courtesy
of the Imperial War Museum*

MAPS IN THE TEXT

Acknowledgements

The author is indebted to the following for permission to quote from books in their copyright: to Messrs. John Murray for *The 56th Division* by Major Dudley Ward; to Messrs. Eyre Methuen for *The Swordbearers* by Correlli Barnett; to Messrs. A.D. Peters & Co. for *The Western Front* by John Terraine, published by Hutchinson & Co.; to Messrs. Hutchinson & Co. for *Warrior* by Lt. Col. Seton Hutchison, *One Way Out* by Sylvia Pankhurst and *My War Memories 1914-18* by General Ludendorff; to Messrs. Constable for 'I have a Rendezvous with Death' by Alan Seeger; to G.T. Sassoon for 'The Menin Arch' by Siegfried Sassoon; to Messrs. Heinemann Ltd for *From Bapaume to Passchendaele* by Philip Gibbs, and to Mrs. M. Gibbs for *Realities of War* by Philip Gibbs; to Charles Edmonds for *A Subaltern's War*; to Messrs. Jonathan Cape for 'Naming of Parts' by Henry Reed; to Mr. Michael Gibson and Macmillan, London and Basingstoke for 'The Golden Room' by Wilfred Gibson; and to Major Kenneth Macksey for *The Shadow of Vimy Ridge*. It has not proved possible to trace several copyright holders, although every effort has been made.

This is a factual story. My original notes on events did not include the names of individuals and as after lapse of time some names cannot be remembered, all the names have been altered.

CHAPTER I

Why Poor Bloody Infantry?

Poor Bloody Infantry was the name given to the foot slogging infantry in the First World War by all other branches of the fighting services. It is not known who first applied that sanguinary label; it was probably a spontaneous expression of sympathy – an acknowledgement of our plight – and as the war went on and on the surviving infantryman accepted it in that spirit. We came to look upon it as a thoroughly justified, well deserved, well earned description, and I feel sure that the following strictly factual story of my war experiences will show why.

It is not intended to be another objective account of how and why particular battles were won or lost with which so many books have adequately dealt, nor is it intended to be similar to those excellent narratives written by Edmund Blunden, Siegfried Sassoon, Henry Williamson and other commissioned officers, but rather an attempt to portray the mental strain of the front line soldier who was inescapably trapped and had to undergo ordeals which often tested him beyond his normal physical and mental powers of endurance. It is essentially a story of how we felt – a story of emotions; and when I say we, I believe I speak for the majority of the amateur volunteer soldiers who constituted the bulk of the P.B.I. in this period of the war.

It is irrefutable that a high standard of morale is the paramount factor in successful warfare, but I am not concerned with victory or defeat in war; my theme is the same as that of Wilfred Owen – the pity of war, and my concern is about the effect of morale on the well being and mental stability of the soldier, because with it he can face extreme hardships and horror with some degree of fortitude; without it, he sinks into a slough of depression and cynicism, with grievances real or imaginary almost to the point of mutiny. Because war histories are more concerned with the strategy of war than with the impact of the fighting on the common soldier, little attention has been paid to this aspect. The question is, why did the morale of the British infantry man reach such a critical low in 1917 and early 1918? It did not, however, sink so low as that of the French *poilu*, the depth of which was clearly shown in the great 1917 mutiny in which fifty divisions were more or less involved. Although I am critical about the class structure of the British army it may be that the discipline engendered by that structure saved us from a similar mutiny after the crime of Passchendaele. The reason, however, for the loss of morale was the same in both armies – muddle, indifference to welfare, and indifference to casualties. Field Marshal Montgomery in his Memoirs writes: 'The frightful casualties appalled me. The so called "good fighting generals" of the war appeared to me to be those who had a complete disregard for human life.' He was so appalled that he was determined that there would never be another Passchendaele. Some critics have said that he was too concerned about possible casualties; be that as it may, the impact and lessons of the First World War helped to make him the foremost commander of the Second World War. His concern for the men and his close contact with all ranks was the key to the high state of morale he invoked.

It was the numbing physical hardship of static trench warfare in the winter and the unimaginative battles of attrition in the spring and summer offensives which changed the enthusiastic volunteer into a disillusioned cynic. This change did not occur in those fortunate enough to be wounded the first time up the line, and so often it was the stories told by these men which allowed war correspondents to give a false picture. The general feeling of the front line troops who had endured and still had to wait for death or the lucky 'blighty' wound was 'to hell with this bloody war – I just want to live'. There were no refresher courses in England lined up for these men, no matter how long they survived. I lasted over twenty months, with one leave after fifteen months, before being gassed, and for me the *Pro Patria Mori* bromide which Wilfred Owen called 'The Old Lie' was soon discarded and finally submerged once and for all in the swamp of Passchendaele.

The last thing I want to do is to discount in any way the part played by the Navy, the Air Force and branches of the Army other than the infantry. All these were necessary to complete the fighting machine, but the plight of the infantry was acknowledged by all; to show why there was a bigger area for hardship and grousing I am obliged to detail and emphasise the difference between the infantry and the rest of the army almost to the point where the critic might ask, 'What did the rest do – it would appear they suffered very little?' Of course they did and with heavy casualties, but in this First World War the infantry man by the very nature of his role and the type of fighting had by far the hardest and most unenviable job.

For example, the mental strain of there being no one else between him and the enemy was very real, not only when going 'over the top' in the large scale offensives, but in the long periods of static trench warfare when the infantry man at night in his short periods of sleep between spells of sentry duty always slept with one eye open because at any time a bomb from a German trench raider might finish him off with practically no warning. Sentry duty meant standing head and shoulders above the parapet exposed to desultory rifle and machine gun fire. Then there were the wiring and patrol parties who went out into No Man's Land less than three hundred yards from the German machine-guns to repair our barbed wire defences, and the raids into German trenches were made only by the infantry. Also the front line soldier suffered much greater physical hardship than any other branch because in winter conditions when trenches and 'bivvies' (shelters excavated in the side of the trench) were flooded as they often were, it meant six days of complete exposure and wading about in water.

Sometimes owing to the close proximity of the Germans there

17

was no supply of hot food or drink. Also, being last in the line of supply, he received less food, less rum ration and in fact less of everything than that accorded to the seven or eight men who were stated to be behind every single infantry man in the front line. One could go on and on and be accused of overstating the case, but there is no overstatement when I say that the mental relief of being in the reserve line a few hundred yards back, knowing that there were troops between oneself and the Germans was immense. It meant a peaceful sleep and how much that was needed.

Even out of the line the infantry man had the worst deal, because he was the footslogger with no transport. An infantry man carried everything he owned in his pack, which with rifle, ammunition, gas mask and other accoutrements weighed little short of eighty pounds. A ten to twelve mile march back to rest billets, particularly in summer when clad in winter clothing with those infernal archaic puttees round the legs was a real test of endurance. Every infantry man would have immediately transferred to any other branch, even to the Vickers machine-gun corps which was closest to him if given the chance, but the chance never came. When you were in, you were in for life, which for the average infantry man was statistically stated to be six months only.

After this exposition it should be possible to understand why everybody called the infantry the P.B.I. – the poor bloody infantry – because that is exactly what they were.

The infantry officer in the line is of course included in the general term P.B.I., but the objective accounts written by commissioned officers from generals to subalterns show little knowledge of the real feelings of the men. This is inevitable, as the life led by the officer and the life led by the ranker were poles apart and there was practically no point of contact. For example even the lowly second lieutenant (subaltern) had a personal servant (batman) to look after him and when in the front line with his platoon he had the most comfortable dugout or bivvy. He had better food, whisky (denied to the troops) and of course no sentry duties or hard physical work, and out of the line he usually had a comfortable billet, often with a bed to sleep in and not the bare floor of a barn or hut. Few of these privileges could have been altered, but the major difference which helped to maintain his morale was that he had the responsibility of being the leader of the thirty or so men of his platoon. Also he had leave at least every six months against fifteen months for the ranker and the chance of a refresher course in England was always there.

It should therefore be obvious why even the life of the platoon officer was very different from that of the men in his platoon; so for the commissioned officer it was a much better war, and when it came to the higher ranks and the staff officers well back from the front it became a much much better war. The terrific contrast between the front line and the various army headquarters, from Divisional H.Q, Corps H.Q, Army H.Q. and finally General Headquarters was well known, and Sir Philip Gibbs, the well known war correspondent, gave a graphic account of life at G.H.Q. Montreuil which he christened the City of Beautiful Nonsense. In his book *Realities of War* he says it was a place

> where the pageantry of war still maintained its old and dead
> tradition ... picturesque, romantic, utterly unreal, as though
> men were playing at war here. The smart society of G.H.Q. was
> best seen at the Officers' Club at Montreuil at dinnertime. It was
> as much like musical comedy as any stage setting of war at the
> Gaiety. A band played ragtime and light music while the
> warriors fed and all these generals and staff officers with their
> decorations and arm bands and polished buttons and crossed
> swords, were waited upon by little W.A.A.C.s with the G.H.Q.
> colours tied up in bows on their hair and khaki stockings under
> their short skirts and fancy aprons. Such chatter! such bursts of
> light hearted laughter! such whisperings of secrets, intrigues and
> scandals in high places! such careless hearted courage when
> British soldiers were being blown to bits, gassed, blinded,
> maimed and shell shocked in places that were far – so very far –
> from G.H.Q.

Gibbs who was the foremost front line war reporter must have been very angry to write in that strain. Later on, commenting on shell shock, he says that shell shock was the worst thing to see. There were generals who said, 'There is no such thing as shell shock. It is cowardice. I would court martial every case.'

Angry? For my part I would like to court martial any general who said that. These generals and staff officers had never been within miles of a modern barrage in which the sheer noise of the shrieking shells and explosions often knocked men silly, destroyed nerve cells and concussed their brains. There are various forms of shell shock – my friend Simpson was unconscious for days. Another man in my platoon suddenly went beserk, charged down the trench with a fixed bayonet and slobbered like a lunatic. Remember, nearly three hundred British soldiers were shot for cowardice in the First World War. Was it always cowardice – who dares to say so?

It may be asked why some sixty years later I feel the need to add yet another account of the war to the many so far written. There have been comparatively few war books written by the non-commissioned soldiers and consequently there has been much truth untold. War is always a filthy business – there may have been glamour at H.Q. but the front line and No Man's Land was for civilised man an obscenity. For most of the time in the front line under fire the soldier is a frightened man and the glossy stories of patient cheerful front line soldiers dying gaily must be refuted.

So here are some extracts from books which are on the shelves of public libraries and are even now being reprinted, and which can be read by the grandchildren of my generation which give them a picture of war quite unlike the war the P.B.I. were in. I feel very strongly about some of the extracts but I realise that even today some men have the 'heroic' attitude to war, particularly the professional soldier who must be trained to kill and some of the enthusiastic volunteers who see in war a 'he-man' challenge which vindicates them as masculine fighting men. I presume the authors are sincere in what they write, but much of what they write does not represent the true picture of the life of the P.B.I.

20

Why P.B.I.?

The first item is a statement made by a Lieutenant Colonel of a machine-gun corps who writes an objective account to correct 'the widely held impression that life on any of the fighting fronts was continuous hell. The author from his diary found that only about one day in twelve was hell. The remaining eleven were spent in "peace time" trenches where nothing except boredom and discomfort happened.'[1]

All I can say is that he was not an infantryman and that this did not apply to my war. My record shows that in the four months November 1916 to February 1917 in the breastworks of the Neuve Chapelle area I did five periods of six days in the front line, five periods of six days in close reserve which meant going up to the breastworks nearly every night with supplies – not one in twelve days but one in two and then on leaving this area for the hoped-for long rest, eight days of continuous marching because the Germans had retreated to the Hindenburg Line and back to the trenches in Arras with the major Arras offensive starting on April 9th 1917.

I could go on with my full twenty months' diary, but I resent statements of this kind which minimise the ordeal of the P.B.I. with talk of nothing except boredom and discomfort eleven twelfths of the time. Even out on rest it was fear – that four letter word so avoided by historians and those writers obsessed with the heroic attitude to war. Yes, it was fear – would one be lucky enough to get the 'blighty' wound – even the loss of a limb the next time up, or would it be the end? Of course that was the nagging thought, how could it be otherwise and there was no escape from this frightfully boring situation.

Here is another priceless remark about boredom. It occurs in an extract from John Terraine's essays *The Western Front 1914/1918* in which Terraine includes a quotation from C. Edmonds' book *A Subaltern's War*. The quotation is as follows:

Fatigue and boredom were probably the worst erosions which the human spirit suffered in the trenches. 'Quite late in the war'

[1] Lt. Col. Howard Green, MC, *The British Army in the First World War*.

said Edmonds, 'I have seen a man go to spend the afternoon in a trench under heavy shell fire because he was bored with sitting in a safe dug out.'

If a man did in fact do that, to use Lord Hailsham's expressive word, he must have been 'bonkers'. Terraine's book borrowed from the public library has been defaced by the word BUNK written large and indelibly in the margin by some irate reader, presumably an old soldier. It is worse than bunk and it is incredible that a front rank historian should make use of such material. Terraine was not in the war and has no knowledge of the mental strain of the front line. Boredom my foot – I must reiterate that *fear* was the worst erosion of the human spirit. In the introduction to this book of essays, Terraine writes of 'the inexhaustible patience and cheerfulness of the troops' – not, I can assure him, of the man in the front line who was fed up to the teeth with his plight; it appears that he has swallowed the Edmonds outlook and that of similar romantic writers hook, line, and sinker.

It was indeed the book by C. Edmonds *A Subaltern's War* which I also found on the shelves of the library that made me realise that time was running out for the First World War veterans and that something must be done to refute the glamorised romantic picture of war. To use Edmonds' own words it is written in 'the rather romantic tone'. It is all that and very readable and dramatic. He says:

It is my hope that the rather romantic tone taken (if I read him right) by that lad who ten years ago was I, may strike responsive chords in the hearts of some old soldiers who are tired of the uniform disillusion of most authors of war books.

Then there is this extract – 'Much has been written of those who died gaily and decently with their faces to the enemy' – and there is more of dying gaily in the epilogue as shown by the following extract:

To die young is by no means an unmitigated misfortune; to die gaily in the unselfish pursuit of what you believe to be a righteous cause is an enviable and not a premature end. Cardinal Mercier expressed this thought still more violently when he said 'how many of these young men who in the impulse of patriotism had the resolution to die well might possibly not have had the resolution to live well'; and as we survivors of the war pass into sordid unheroic middle age, it is not pity that we feel for those who died on the field of honour. God grant that we may be as lucky in the occasion of our death, and may meet it with a soldier's gay courage.

When I read this junk I am almost speechless and the quotation of Cardinal Mercier is a gem. The old bromide of 'Pie in the sky when you die' dished out on a very large platter.

In dealing with a German counter attack the same author writes:

... I saw straight to the front and a hundred yards away a crowd of men running towards us in grey uniforms. Picking up another rifle I joined him in pouring rapid fire into this counter attack. We saw one at least drop, to Walker's rifle I think, then noticed that they were running with their hands up. Laughing, we emptied our magazines into them in spite of that. ...

The saints preserve us from those who kill laughing and talk of dying gaily. I saw many die but none gaily. It must have been a different war.

I would like to quote from one more book, particularly as it leads into the effect of lack of communication on morale. This book is *Warrior*, written by Lieutenant Colonel Seton Hutchison, commander of 33rd Division Machine-Gun Corps. This is an exciting, dynamic and very readable book with graphic descriptions of battles and conditions but which also sets out to glorify the 'Warrior', whom he rightly describes as the footslogger of the infantry – the poor bloody infantry, he calls them. He was a

soldier before the war, a regular army officer whose profession, I suppose, entitles him to be enthusiastic about certain aspects of the war. His last prose line in the book is 'Here upon the highest peak of human history yet unafraid Warrior stands'. He also says, '... I confess unashamedly to having enjoyed the war ... those four tragic thrilling happy years'. This may be a professional.soldier's point of view but it was certainly not that of the infantryman.

There is also another revealing comment in this book which gives a clear indication of the class ridden structure of the British army. He says:

> The officer who has learned his business, not always an easy task; and who, beyond this, had triumphed in the far more difficult matter of human psychology, of men and motives, did in fact know a great deal more of the character and thoughts, conscious and subconscious of the private soldier under battle conditions, than the average private soldier could possibly understand for himself.

He understood psychology so well that when he found British soldiers, stragglers in retreat in the battle of the Lys he says, 'We discovered in the Belle Croix estaminet beside the mill a crowd of stragglers, fighting drunk. We routed them out and with a machine-gun trained on them sent them forwards towards the enemy. They perished to a man.'

This comment about the superiority of the officer class in the British regimental set-up where the men were almost a different species could not possibly have been made by an Australian or Canadian officer. In the practically classless Commonwealth forces, where the educational system had not separated the classes, there was ample communication between the officers and men, while in the British Army it was sadly lacking. What a difference it made to the morale and fighting quality of the men. The German fear of being up against the Commonwealth troops was fully justified by results. They were not necessarily better men, but they were better trained as an integral unit.

In his book *The Shadow of Vimy Ridge* Major Kenneth Macksey writes:

With them there was a wholesale sharing of knowledge, illustrated by the remarks of a Canadian Staff Officer, Capt. D.C. MacIntyre: 'We placed absolute trust in our men, and took them entirely into our confidence. Instead of issuing a few maps to the officers, every single man was taken to see large scale maps and a clay model reproduction of the battlefield and its objectives. We were confident that no one would desert and divulge information, and no one did.'

In the British Army there was great reluctance to share knowledge with the men and Major Macksey emphasises this point when he writes:

There was a gulf in communications between officers and men, the one often not explaining to the other what was going on. As a result there were repeated instances in which the loss of officers paralysed subsequent actions because the men were not aware of the plan.

In twenty months, even as an N.C.O. I saw no map of any description. In twenty months I saw our Brigadier once only and that was when he was in General Haking's retinue. No red-banded Staff Officer was ever seen by me in the front line or even in the reserve line. They knew nothing about conditions and were completely out of contact with the men. No less a person than Field Marshal Montgomery endorsed this lack of communication when he wrote, 'There was little contact between the generals and the soldiers'.

It is surely relevant to show that this same blight permeated the Navy which suffered even more from the grip of a privileged class. Correlli Barnett in his book *The Swordbearers* writes, 'Drawing most of its officers from one per cent of the nation the Royal Navy never tapped the great reservoir of urban middle class talent that made Scheer's fleet so well educated and so intelligent.' Admiral Fisher in 1906 said, 'Surely we are drawing our Nelsons from too narrow a class'. This same class had the paramount control over the design of our ships and guns, so that Jellicoe was obliged to say in 1914, 'It is highly dangerous to consider our ships as a whole are superior or even equal fighting machines,' this must have been brought home to Beatty with some force in the Battle of Jutland when he lost the *Queen Mary, Invincible, Defence,* and *Warrior* to the superior marksmanship and shells of the German fleet, and caused him to make the often quoted remark 'There seems to be something wrong with our bloody ships today', and there was. With twice the number of ships, we lost 112,000 tons with about 7,000 casualties and the Germans 62,000 tons and 2,900 casualties. The Germans claimed a victory and well they might. Correlli Barnett writes in his book:

The weaknesses of British naval technology at Jutland were in part owing to the close personal relations of private firms and the Admiralty officers (who often joined the boards of such firms on retirement) and the relatively small number of firms who could undertake the work. Thus, really ruthless, independent testing and rejection of poor designs or poor quality were humanly very difficult ...

The navy reflected social rather than functional values; preoccupation with tradition rather than technology.

It was a closed shop.

It may be asked what have these observations about the class structure of the forces to do with the P.B.I., but since the morale of the infantryman is the major theme of the account which follows, lack of communication is a very relevant factor.

In the ensuing pages of this story will be found what some will consider unpatriotic sentiments, a too cynical attitude about war aims and the conduct of the war and too much grousing about conditions. In Siegfried Sassoon's words we were 'The doomed conscripted unvictorious ones', most of whom became 'the unheroic dead who fed the guns'.

Yes, despite the stiff upper lips we were often frightened men who did not want to die for their country or for any other cause – but just wanted to live, live, live. There are always men and women who are willing to risk their lives and even give their lives for a high ideal, but what on earth was the high ideal in the First World War. In the whole of history, this was probably the war that should not have happened because it proved nothing and settled nothing. It need not have happened, but the war game balance of power tactics played by the great powers in the first thirteen years of the twentieth century and the enormous but profitable expenditure in armaments in the five years before 1914, made the war inevitable. In the power game, a war to bolster up the tottering Austrian Empire and to save the face of her German backer, was a necessity.

When one reads the many histories of the origin of the First World War one is appalled by the devious diplomacy of this power game – the Triple Alliance – the Triple Entente – which was played by the men in power in all the nations concerned. Compared with the total population of a country the men in power, i.e. statesmen, the leaders of the armed forces, the directors of armament firms and producers of war material, are numerically extremely small. These, however, are the people who make the decisions about war and peace – these are the people we designate as 'the country', England, France, Germany, Russia etc. They do not of course constitute the true country which is that amorphous mass of population on a much lower standard of organisation and intelligence who, brainwashed with slogans from the powerful vested interest minority, become the cannon fodder of war. 'Theirs is not to reason why – theirs is but to do and die' and that they did in millions.

CHAPTER 2

Patriotic Hysteria

What a long way removed is this attitude from the enthusiasm of August 1914. Men rushed to join up – 30,000 in one day and in the first twelve months two million volunteers had enlisted. It cannot be easy for the present generation to understand the war hysteria which swept through Europe on the outbreak of war. For a decade, the rivalry between Germany and England for world markets and consequent world power had been fomented by the vested interests, the press, and politicians of both sides. Songs and music have always been potent forces for rousing emotions. There was the song 'Let me like a soldier fall' which was carried over from the Victorian era and the Boer War. The opening lines ran something like this:

> Let me like a soldier fall upon some foreign plain.
> My breast expanded meets the ball that shall wipe out every stain.

This was not a comic song but sung in many drawing rooms and concert halls with great fervour and deadly seriousness. Another song which was very popular at that time was:

> We are sons of the sea, all British born
> Sailing every ocean laughing foes to scorn,
> They may build their ships my lads and think they know the game,
> But they can't beat the lads of the bulldog breed
> Who made old England's name.

As a schoolboy I sang that with gusto and 'they' were always the Germans – the Germans who had stolen a march on us with their new Dreadnought battleships. 'We won't wait – we want eight' was the reply of the press and public to Asquith's 'Wait and see' policy. We were not alone in our belligerency – in Germany, in Heidelberg and other universities dedicated duel scarred students toasted *Der Tag* with patriotic fervour and eagerly awaited its dawning. My country right or wrong was the creed of the peoples of Europe.

At school we were fully indoctrinated with the British Empire cult. A map of the world at that time would show about one fifth coloured red – the British Empire; I well remember Empire Day celebrations when with a thousand or more school children dressed in red white or blue smocks I helped to form a huge Union Jack at the Bristol City football ground. Clara Butt, the famous contralto, sang 'Land of Hope and Glory' from the grandstand, while we contributed the Empire Day anthem 'Flag of Britain proudly waving over many distant seas' and Kipling's Recessional 'Lord God of Hosts be with us yet, lest we forget' with the stunning line about 'Lesser breeds without the law'. As I grew older I often thought of the arrogance of that line. Whose law – God's or the British.

In 1914 the British knew that they were the foremost nation in the world, not only because of naval power but in moral development. Our standards were higher; our history books assured us that we did the right things in the right way, not how much of the Empire had been taken from the 'lesser breeds' by conquest and exploitation. No nation's history books tell the whole truth; in fact the school history books of all nations were so nationally biased that lies, particularly lies of omission were numerous. This colouring of history, old and new was and is the policy of all nations, so that when a crisis affecting the nation arises, the masses – 'the country' can usually be persuaded that what the men in power say is right. It might appear from this criticism that I am anti-British but Britain is the only place I wish to live in. It is the music centre of the world and foremost in literature and the arts. Few countries can offer such a combination of lovely villages, old churches and buildings, varied scenery, varied climate, and the cosy atmosphere of the British inns and pubs is unique. It is said that truth is many sided and those who tell experienced, unpalatable truths are often pilloried for the telling. We criticise because we care and the criticism in this story is a measure of that.

In 1914 all the belligerents believed that they were fighting in a just cause, in defence of their country – they were being attacked – their freedom was at stake, and all the various Christian churches in the various Christian countries prayed to their national God for victory. What a dilemma for God! The propaganda, exaggerations and falsehoods broadcast in the first decade of the twentieth century provided fuel for the holocaust (9,000,000 dead, 21,000,000 wounded) which was detonated at Sarajevo in June 1914 when a young student, Princeps, (now a national hero) assassinated the Austrian Grand Duke and his wife.

The following autobiographical account of two and a half years of war will show how the first naive enthusiasm turned to disillusion. It is not a story overfull with the blood and guts of casualty horrors. Also it is not a story to show how heroically we survived – we were not heroes, but trapped, frustrated, and often doomed men. It is a journey down the memory lane of over half a century ago; the marvel is that one can still see events as though they happened yesterday. It is a simple story typify' ig the thoughts and emotions of most of the P.B.I. I feel that something must be done to counter the glamorised picture of war appearing in articles and books. Time has almost run out for the survivors of the First World War, and the 'truth untold' should be told even at this late stage in the hope that the younger generation will see through the propaganda with which they will be bombarded if the Third World War begins to get under way.

Here then is the story.

CHAPTER 3

Joining the P.B.I.

When war was delcared I was on holiday in my native town Cheltenham and saw the first contingent of local Territorials march down the beautiful tree lined promenade on a warm summer day to the cheers of an enthusiastic crowd. A military band and marching soldiers are always an inspiring sight, but this was for real – they were off to war and how we youngsters envied them. The excitement in that Cotswold town was infectious. In Germany the young Germans went off flower decked and to the cheers of the crowds of handkerchief waving civilians. It was so inspiring – like the rest of Europe they were marching to victory – they had been born, cared for, and educated just for this moment.

With my uncle in a local pub that night, I listened to the pundits saying that the Germans couldn't shoot, that a German battleship had been sunk in the Channel, and that the war would be over before Christmas. It was good to be alive on such a day, but so disappointing to be only seventeen as I had eighteen months to wait and the war would be over long before that. I was a very junior Civil Servant in the Scottish Office, Dover House, Whitehall with the War Office a few hundred yards away and at the back, the large Horse Guards Square; what a vantage point during the next few months to watch the comings and goings of the top brass service men and politicians.

In October I was transferred to the Board of Trade Westminster, and although many youngsters were enlisting under age I could not get away – no release until nineteen. This was very frustrating because my friends in the digs, Williams and Watson, although in the War Office, were allowed to go. It was the glamorous City of London Rough Riders for them and how they enjoyed clanking about wearing their jingling dress spurs.

This was most depressing for me and I thought that the thrill of being a despatch rider might just get me on level terms with them, so I made my preliminary application ready for my call up. The snag was how could I learn to ride a motor bike in time! And to tell the truth that was it – glamour – to be in uniform – to take part in a great adventure was as much the reason for so many youths joining up as any sense of patriotism. For most, even when they thought about death on the battlefield the old bromide that 'it will never happen to me' was the soporific.

In 1916 with the knowledge that the war would not be a short one there was increasing pressure for more volunteers in order to avoid hated conscription. Recruiting sergeants interrupted cinema shows with lurid descriptions of German brutality. I was in the Blue Halls cinema, Hammersmith, when a purported eye witness account was given by a sergeant of the killing of women and children just for the fun of it and in the war hysteria of the day we believed it. The truth is we wanted to believe it.

This campaign of atrocity stories was a standard method of arousing the emotions of the indignant civilian, in the hope that in a wave of patriotic enthusiasm he would dash off to the nearest recruiting office. The most effective recruiting agents, however, were the women and girls who distributed white feathers to men not in uniform and not wearing a war service badge. From stage shows actresses sang numerous patriotic songs and the most popular one was:

We don't want to lose you but we think you ought to go,
For your King and your country both need you so,
We shall want you and miss you but with all our might and
main,
We shall cheer you, bless you, kiss you, when you come back
again.

Breastwork repairs in the Laventie area, showing a typical 'bivvy'

Day sentry duty in the breastworks with the inadequate box periscope

Laventie area: a Lewis Gun team filling sandbags

Cleaning the Lewis Gun. The photograph shows a sandbag camouflaged periscope

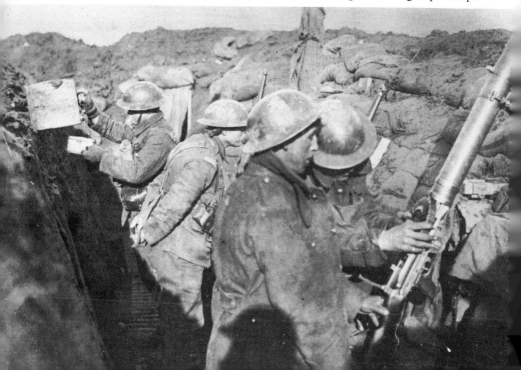

The women certainly did their bit by forcing the not too enthusiastic men into the Services. However the rush of volunteers slackened, and towards the end of 1915 the number of recruits fell below those essential for the conduct of the war. To stave off conscription Lord Derby introduced a scheme which invited all men between the ages of 18 and 41 to enlist and be called up in age groups, unmarried before married.

I enlisted under this scheme in October 1915 with my father, in Bristol where I was on sick leave with my arm in a sling; I had managed to get a wrist broken when playing football. The Conscription Act was, however, passed very soon afterwards.

In March 1916 I thought I ought to get busy and join a battalion of my choice because I should be nineteen before the month was out. I suppose the natural place for a civil servant would have been in the Civil Service Rifles but I wanted something different, so I thought I would try to join one of the City of London battalions; at the headquarters of the London Rifle Brigade I was interviewed by a sergeant regarding my school, occupation etc. Noticing that I wore glasses he said that despite the fact that my eyesight might be good with them I must pass the battalion test, so upstairs I went where a corporal gave me an eye test which I failed by one line without glasses.

I then tried the Honourable Artillery Company, a few yards away, and again all was well except for the eye test. It was all very frustrating. About two weeks later I received an official notice to appear at the White City, Shepherds Bush, where there was a very motley crowd and we were treated quite roughly.

After the routine medical examination I was taken to another room to take the enlistment oath, but I protested that I had already joined under the Derby Scheme at Bristol some months previously. Then I was told for the first time that I had been called up as a conscript, that they had no record of my enlistment and that I would be posted to the regular army that day. After a lot of argument during which I surprised myself and the army personnel present by refusing point blank to take the oath, an officer then appeared but I still protested, particularly as we were all to be posted to the regular army that day. Eventually I saw the officer in charge, a sympathetic major who gave me twenty four hours to join the regiment of my choice. I was in a real fix, but decided to try again for the London Rifle Brigade. Hopefully, I thought there may be different staff on duty, so not wearing glasses back I went, but unfortunately it was the same sergeant who asked the same questions and got slightly varied answers.

Then, looking at me closely he said, 'Haven't you been here before?'

'No,' I said, lying as calmly as possible.

'All right' he said, 'go upstairs for an eye and hearing test.'

The test card had been carelessly left on view, and getting the new corporal in general conversation for a few moments I managed to memorise my fail line and that was that. I passed the test without glasses and as my sight was better than average with glasses I was accepted. Joining up had been quite a shambles, but having enlisted voluntarily I was determined to join a battalion of my choice even by subterfuge. What a start for my army career! In fact it was really a good start as I was very fortunate in joining a first class territorial battalion where I found congenial companions and where I had exceptional luck to survive a long period of front line service.

A few days were spent at the Bunhill Row Drill Hall learning how to march, form fours etc., and getting fitted out with uniform. Mine were far from being a Savile Row fit, and with my small size I looked a long way from being every inch a soldier. Then we were off to Fovant, a small village about ten miles from Salisbury. What nostalgic memories Fovant conjures up. The six months at Fovant were the best part of my army life. For one thing the camp was situated in a lovely quiet part of Wiltshire and on one side of the camp was a high, smooth grass-covered escarpment. I am not sure that the large regimental badges cut in the chalk hillside with much hard labour was an improvement on nature, but I suppose it denoted a praiseworthy competitive effort of 'Anything you can do we can do better', between the battalions and helped to maintain *esprit de corps.* How top brass overworked those words we found out in the ensuing months, and survivors in ensuing years. Forty years later when passing through this area I saw that the badges were still there being preserved by volunteer effort.

Well, there we were, thirty white-faced enthusiastic volunteer 'rookies' and we were all housed in one large wooden hut. We were not white-faced with apprehension – that would come later – but the contrast between us and the sun tanned two or three months trained veterans was very marked. We were a good mixture, about one third married, and with roughly similar views and standards we soon became a congenial happy crowd. The training was tough – very tough. We could have managed the weaponry in a few weeks but the main task was to get everyone hardened up and fit to carry a full pack of about eighty pounds including rifle and ammunition for a twenty mile march. Apart from the railway for long distances there was never any transport for the P.B.I. It was footslogging with a vengeance but how fit we became and felt on top of the world. It was blisters and boots, boots and blisters, boots were certainly made for walking until at last even a small 'un like me could carry the full pack on long distance marches.

Not content with the intensive training I took on boxing, walking races, football, and cross-country running at which I was quite good and managed to get into the battalion team. It was a lovely spring and summer – a never to be forgotten season of high endeavour and it would have been hard to find a more enthusiastic crowd. It is not an exaggeration to say that the spirit of that summer was caught in Rupert Brooke's lines:

Now God be thanked who has matched us with His hour,
And caught our youth and wakened us from sleeping.

Yet only six months later in the Combles attack September 1916 the first time up the line this happy crowd was smashed up and at least half were killed or wounded.

35

The competition between platoons was intense and it was woe betide any man who let the side down. I am afraid I did over a trace of dust on my shelf which a young officer found when passing his finger over it. Fantastic I suppose, but that was the standard. Spit and polish later called 'bull' was carried to unjustifiable extremes. On Saturday night we had first class concerts in the large dining hall with all ranks in attendance. There was plenty of talent, some professional, and I can still remember Thomas, a fine tenor, singing the sentimental ballads of the day such as 'Take thou this Rose', 'The Garden of your Heart' and 'Sincerity'. We lived for the day with little thought for the time ahead. Why think of the morrow when we had no idea what we were in for.

Some of the training was very boring particularly rifle instruction and somehow Henry Reed's poem 'Naming of Parts' written at a later date always recalls those boring lessons. The first verse is:

Today we have naming of parts. Yesterday,
We had daily cleaning. And tomorrow morning
We shall have what to do after firing. But today
Today we have naming of parts. Japonica
Glistens like coral in all the neighbouring gardens,
And today we have naming of parts.

In this story there are a number of extracts from poetry, because as a lover of poetry I feel with Victor Gollancz who said somewhere:

The poet is a man who sees something ineffable behind the things of this world and seeing it as beauty makes an effort to express it in words; in words that even as they come make the vision itself a little clearer to himself and others.

Then there are Wilfred Owen's words, not so much about beauty but the truth of war, when of his war poetry he wrote:

My subject is war and the pity of war. The Poetry is in the pity. All the poets can do today is to warn.

36

The tragic gloomy words of Wilfred Owen could not, however, have been applied to this training period.

In the centre of the camp was the Square where for the next few months we were going to be licked into shape with 'left right, left right, pick it up – form fours' – on the left form close column of platoon, and then there was physical training with 'On the hands down – down stretch, down stretch – one two – one two – stick that arse in', until having been shouted at, bullied, with comments of 'some mothers do have 'em' came the welcome 'Dismiss'.

Then the shower and the flop down on the straw mattress three plank bed for a short rest before night operations. While these showed the danger of being silhouetted against the sky line much of our field training operations were a waste of time because for us there was to be no open warfare; but later on in life I did find the signal to close – a semi-circular motion of the arm, then straight above the head and the fist being brought straight down to the head – was most useful at the seaside when my young daughters were straying too far!

The biggest time-waster, however, was the bayonet drill as not one hundredth of one per cent of the infantry in the 1914/18 war ever used a bayonet. With a bullet in the rifle and a Mills bomb, why use the bayonet? If ordinary human standards are anything to go by, the drill was really obscene. We were instructed to charge sacks marked with discs denoting head, eyes and heart and we had to yell like maniacs as we struck; then foot on, and the withdrawal of the bayonet always had to be with a twisting movement to disembowel, then on with an upward jab into the throat, the butt being swung into the privates. That was the routine drill and we did it hundreds of times and the main idea must have been to create the offensive spirit and change the normal person into a bloodthirsty murderer.

In the official notes about the need for bayonet fighting, the words 'to encourage the lust for blood' were used. What a high ideal for twentieth century man. Perhaps murder is too strong a word, one only kills the enemy – this nameless unknown enemy

37

which your 'country' – that is the men in power who make and declare war – tells you that it is your patriotic duty to kill. These, however, were not Fovant thoughts where we all yelled and jabbed with the best, but Passchendaele thoughts after the shock of the salient.

Training culminated in the firing range test where everyone tried to obtain the coveted marksman badge, but usually only succeeded in being rated as a first-class shot. The final effort was the throwing of a live Mills bomb. This was the most efficient bomb of the war in killing power, but a thirty yards throw was about the limit for a first-class bomber. The German stick bomb could be thrown much further and their egg bombs like large stones had an even longer range. The Mills bomb had a serrated cast iron case with a lever flush with the case and held down by a split pin. The split pin was withdrawn and when the bomb was thrown the handle flew off causing detonation and five seconds later the bomb exploded. The 'wind up' and the general nerves engendered by this simple exercise were rather remarkable. Pity the poor officer in the bombing bay where a nervous 'rooky' might drop the bomb or hit the parapet with it. The worst job was going out to look for a dud which had not exploded; we had our tragedy when a lad stepped on a bomb and it blew him up. I well remember the sad parents at the military funeral we gave him.

By this time we had all heard about the heavy casualties of the battalion's 1st July attack at Gommecourt and there were now a number of overseas men wounded earlier in the year back with the battalion for fresh training and yet no matter what we were told about the hardships and the horrors of the fighting we simply did not want to know; we had to see it for ourselves. Like Norwegian lemmings we were all keyed up and raring to go – not into the sea, but over the sea and for so many with the same fate in store.

In retrospect it fully proved to me how difficult it is to transmit physical experiences so I am resigned to the fact that whatever I write now about this aspect may have little impact – all I can hope for is to reiterate and reiterate the folly of war by giving a general picture of the day to day life, hopes, and fears of the P.B.I. I know that the poets do it much better but every little helps. I also realise that for the young people of today the First World War is ancient history – sixty years back the Crimean War was just that for me when I was about seventeen years old.

August came all too soon and then draft leave. On returning to camp from leave I was challenged by the guard who asked me where I had come from. The reaction when I said 'Bristol' left me rather dazed for I was immediately marched to a hut on the outskirts of the camp where I joined a physical training sergeant and two other men. When I asked what on earth was going on the sergeant said, 'A sailor is in hospital in Bristol suffering from bubonic plague and we are to be isolated for about three weeks'. It was a terribly boring three weeks as we were treated like lepers with our food being left outside the hut and the plates etc., being sterilised before being returned. We played games until we were sick of them.

Meanwhile my platoon and all my friends had gone off to France and I suppose that was the beginning of my luck which stayed with me all through the war so that I eventually managed to survive for over twenty months in France in a front line infantry battalion, when the average life of an infantry private was less than six months. That Bristol sailor kept me out of the Somme attack where so many of my friends were killed – a fantastic million to one chance.

It was soon draft leave again and again I was held up, this time for a special medical examination as the new doctor did not like my heart action. It was of course heart strain, because coupled with the vigorous training I had been selected for the battalion cross country team – one thing I could do pretty well. It was the big Southern Counties event held at Fovant which did the extra damage, as after about three miles my shoe lace broke and it was then a struggle to make up the distance and stay with the team. To make things worse I mistook the crowd at the beginning of the village for the finishing line – spurted – overtook one or two and then found I had another half mile to do. I did it, but passed out. It was not my day. My disorganised heart action (D.A.H.) which was quite genuine and in normal times would have put me into Grade 2 stayed with me for most of the war. I remember after some time in the front line I went sick with rather a severe bout of D.A.H. and with luck it might have got me out of the hell hole of the trenches but this did not happen. When right up in the front line one had to be very third rate to get away. What a cowardly confession the stiff-upper-lippers will say at my comment, 'With luck I might have got away'. What a contrast to a war correspondent's story of a wounded man who was purported to have said, 'I wouldn't have missed it for the world, I'm sorry I was wounded – I would like to go back and be in it at the end'. What utter bilge and sop for the home front. Under the wretched conditions which prevailed in this period of the war most infantry men wanted to get away from the front line. Attempts to go sick with no sound reason was called 'swinging the lead'. Why was trench feet made a court martial offence? Because by neglect it was so easy to contract it.

CHAPTER 4

France

Draft night, October 11th 1916, was the usual drinking bout and my throat was sore the next day with the repeated choruses of 'I've gotta a motta always merry and bright', 'Here's to good old whisky, drink it down', 'The old bass bottle', and some unprintable ditties which were routine procedure on draft nights. Another peculiar symptom of the draft fever was that of having the shortest of short hair cuts – almost a shaving. Some did, some didn't, I didn't. Those who did, looked horrible – I suppose it was a 'goodbye to all that' gesture. Unfortunately I was with relative strangers as all my close friends had gone to France weeks before.

The next morning it was the Fovant station farewells and I noticed our tough Regimental Sergeant Major had tears in his eyes. He knew what we were in for, particularly as the 1st July Somme survivors were already back. I remember on that sunny October morning on the short journey to Southampton looking at the English fields and hedgerows and wondering now whether I would ever see them again, but it was probably because I was on my own amongst relative strangers that my thoughts took a rather sober line.

By the time we reached the goods sheds at Southampton it was pouring with rain and a south west gale was blowing. We were to have made a crossing to Le Havre that night but a submarine was reported in the Channel, and so a miserable night and day was spent in the shed. The next night we went on board the small troop transport, and in heavy seas with a destroyer on each side we were off. More than half the men on that crowded ship were seasick, but I was one of the lucky ones and I spent the night on deck behind a funnel drenched with spray. It was a miserable wet dawn when we landed but we were very excited at being on foreign soil and as we marched through the town the fit ones were singing as though going on holiday. It was a long march to the camp which was situated below the notorious 'Pimple' plateau, the final training ground. We were crowded into bell tents and I thought it strange that after two years of war a decent camp had not been erected.

Then there were three weeks of what I thought at the time was pretty awful, as much mentally as physically; but it was of course paradise to what was to follow in the next two years. The Pimple was reached by a long uphill march and with full pack one felt pretty tired before commencing the day's training on the assault courses. The instructors were mostly hard bitten regular soldiers who had been up the line and who were known as canaries because they wore yellow arm bands. They tried to put the fear of God into us 'rookies' and why not? Their job, their duty, was to make us more efficient fighters. Some almost had apoplexy at our rifle brigade style of marching. Rifle battalions were used to 140 to the minute jogging parade step and we were continually harassed on our woebegone efforts to march with the sedate slow Guards step. The remarks such as 'What a bloody mob – what a moshup – my God Bill did you ever see anything like it – left roight, lef roight, pick it up you toy soldiers' did absolutely nothing for our ego.

We were on the Pimple day after day – all day – with only sandwiches and tea, being driven like animals over assault courses with fixed bayonets, charging sacks, jumping in and out of trenches, and climbing over palisades. An ambulance was in attendance as sometimes there were minor casualties when a man might slip and stick his bayonet into another man's leg or backside.

This tough physical training was only to be expected – we were not on a pleasure jaunt. Loneliness was the trouble. The old battalion was home, and it was lonely outside. At the Havre camp it dawned for the first time that as a footslogging private I was on

42

my own. I mattered to myself and to no one else; as for the rest I was just a number on my identity disc 301258, and that was all.

This narrative now begins to sound like a perpetual grouse. Were there any redeeming features? I am afraid not many, and it was soon clear that some very large reserve of enthusiastic patriotism would be needed to maintain the first fine careless enlistment rapture. The main pastime in the evening was 'housey housey', now called Bingo, played in a large roofed in area, at one penny per line or two pennies for the full card. It was an army regulation that every evening before the start anyone could take part in the ceremony of cutting cards to be in the group who would take charge that night. The team of six to eight always shared in a rake off benefit as on each round a percentage was deducted for those in charge. The percentage was not fixed and one night when a particularly acquisitive team was in charge with poor pay outs there was almost a riot. Of course this was a monopoly run by a well seasoned group of old sweats and it was probably more than your life was worth to attempt to cut in. This was the only public gambling game allowed in the army; all others such as the notorious 'Crown and Anchor' meant severe trouble for those caught.

Then came the final medical examination and another first time rejection. The tough training on the Pimple had not improved my heart action. I was re-examined presumably by a specialist two days later. It was thorough and after answering a number of questions he allowed me to remain in the A.I. category. It must have been marginal and the strange thing was that although I had every opportunity to tip the balance, and I believe I could easily have done so, I did nothing to assist my rejection. It was not that I felt some definite urge to kill Germans or that I had such a high sense of patriotism that I wanted to die for my country; it was simply that apart from curiosity – I wanted to see the front line – probably above all I wanted to be able to say that I had been right in it.

I believe that this apparently small point gives a most important clue to the subconscious thinking and subsequent actions of the

43

volunteer soldier. I am sure that this urge to be right in it – to bear witness about the front line was the way thousands and thousands of volunteers found themselves in that front line, but after only one attack or even only the first six days in a sodden rat ridden trench with the exercise of running for life from the 'minnies' (very large trench mortar) every day, every one of them would have taken a cushy job away from that place of fear.

So about three weeks after landing in France the moment came to resume our journey to the front line and for so many of the P.B.I. it was a one way ticket only.

We entrained in goods wagons labelled '8 *chevaux* 40 *hommes*'. My train journeys in France were always in these French Pullmans. Fortunately our battalion draft was off to join our own battalion on the Somme. Sometimes drafts were shunted to any battalion. We had an overnight stop at a camp on the banks of the Seine at Rouen. Next day at some station halt Simpson my friend of the old original Fovant platoon joined us to take us to Picquiny where the battalion had been pulled out of the line. He gave me details about the Combles attack of 26th September when about half of my Fovant platoon had been wiped out. He was very much changed – he had had a shock and I am sure he would have jumped at the chance of a transfer from the P.B.I. I knew him well and he had a different look – hunted – frightened – I don't know. Perhaps we all looked like that after a big attack. At Picquiny I was posted to Simpson's platoon in which platoon I stayed for the next twenty months in France. We were billeted in an old draughty warehouse with three tier bunks made of chicken run wire netting and articles not kept on the ground sheets were liable to drop on the chaps below; then things really hotted up. It was very cold with only one blanket and when I grumbled about the cold, Simpson said, 'Just you wait – this is Paradise'.

We had a few uneventful days at Picquiny when I became acquainted with the rest of the platoon and other N.C.O.s and officers of the battalion. I thought our Colonel was a complete picture book fighting soldier; handsome with a Kaiser Wilhelm moustache and five gold wound stripes on his sleeve and he rode a beautiful black polo pony. Of the company captains I suppose Stayman was the most colourful; he was one of the original peace time battalion privates who had won the D.C.M. in 1915. He had an excellent parade voice, was good looking, and popular with the rankers because he always seemed to know what he was doing and exuded confidence.

Most of the rankers in this battalion were of the same social and educational standard as the officers and good understanding and *esprit de corps* was the basis of the disciplinary system. It worked well until 1918 when most of the originals having become casualties, these methods were not understood by the replacements and orthodox disciplinary methods had to be introduced. I soon discovered how fortunate I was to have joined this battalion with its high standards and spirit of co-operation which, despite the general loss of morale in 1917, meant that in spite of everything we stood together and did not let each other down or the side down. I can only speak for my Company but we had first class N.C.O.s of good understanding from the Sergeant Major downwards and that meant so much in the wretched conditions under which we lived.

A few more days went by and then we were told we were going to the village of Huppy some twenty miles back where the battalion had been billeted before the September attack. A one day march was planned and twenty miles with full pack and rifle was going to be tough. March discipline was always rigorously imposed and it consisted of marching for one hour, then ten minutes halt, then marching fifty minutes and ten minutes halt and so on. I suppose the average speed was just over two miles an hour. A few fell out, and most of us were flat out by the time we reached Huppy – a lovely little village. We were there just four days and we were completely browned off when we were told that we had to leave immediately for the Ypres salient, the worst spot on the whole front. How the mood changed.

I found later that for the experienced soldier this was always so. A nice quiet village – the war is oh so far away and then the news

45

comes that you are moving off for a big stunt or a lively part of the front. That is the time for the tummy feeling – the quiet depression, the look of doom. As you move nearer the line that mood passes – it becomes a little better and there is a more fatalistic attitude. After all your name has got to be on the shell or bullet and if it isn't you will be all right, or perhaps the long hoped for blighty wound will materialise, and be bad enough to get back to England but not too bad.

Well, we were off again; a few miles march to a rail head and then into the French Pullmans. We spent one horribly cold, uncomfortable night in the trucks in the railway yard and the next day we reached Hazebrouck. The good news was that we were not going to the salient but to the Richbourg l'Avoué, Laventie, Neuve Chapelle area which was the battlefield in the abortive 1915 offensive.

More marching, the sound of guns nearer and nearer, and our Company finished up in a little village called Paradis, and that is what it was. Our billet was on the upper floor of a barn with clean straw and the farm was run by a sympathetic farmer and his wife who supplied us with coffee and new French bread. As always, French bread was delicious but in a few months' time French ration regulations made it an offence to sell it. In this area farms were occupied, and all the normal life went on to within about three or four miles of the front line. There appears to have been a tacit agreement in the period of winter warfare between the British and the Germans by which shelling was limited to about three miles on each side of No Man's Land – in fact the area covered by shell fire was often reduced to about a mile.

CHAPTER 5

The Breastworks

Although the battalion was tired with marching we only had two days' rest and then moved to the reserve positions. We soon had the order to march in battle formation, that is about fifty yards between each platoon. This was when the war seemed very near and the first-timers were wondering how they would behave if a shell came over. I had no idea what I would do except that I would watch the old soldiers' reactions. This was completely flat country – flat fields with innumerable ditches for drainage and willow trees dotted about. Camouflage netting on tall poles screened the road from German observation balloons. In the damp dull weather this flat scenery was most depressing.

Eventually we came to some cross roads at Croix Barbée and my platoon was put into an almost intact large barn, but now there were no straw or blankets. However with clothes kept on, an overcoat for a blanket, a nobbly haversack for a pillow, one soon got used to sleeping on bare earth. It was over twelve months before I again slept in a bed and it is really amazing how easily the trappings of comfort can be dispensed with. In the next four or five months of winter warfare sleep was a luxury – sleep, food, and safety became heaven on earth.

The next day we were told that we were taking over the front line opposite the Bois du Biez which had been christened by the army 'Mystery Wood' in which a company of Gurkhas disappeared in the 1915 Neuve Chapelle attack. Our corporal had been up to the front line to contact the troops we were to relieve and he said that we were going to have a very quiet time with practically no action on either side.

In this area daylight relief was the routine, so we packed our gear and wearing overcoats we proceeded up a muddy road and after about half a mile entered a communication trench usually known as the C.T. It was a rum sort of trench because it only went down about two feet and it was built up to about another five feet with earth filled sandbags held in position with latticed wood and chicken run wire. It zigzagged every few yards to localise shell bursts. On the bottom of the trench were duck boards i.e. two six to nine feet wooden joists with pieces of wood latticed across and these rested on short posts which were driven into the waterlogged clay. There must have been hundreds of thousands of duck boards used on the Western Front. They were absolutely necessary to keep the army mobile, otherwise feet and legs would become stuck in gluey mud. Every so often there was a deep sump hole in which surface water hopefully drained and in this area many of the sump holes contained dead rats which had fallen in and drowned.

C.T. travelling was always tiring and exasperating particularly at night. The hazards in moving along a C.T. were plentiful and there was a constant stream of messages being passed as one moved clumsily along with pack and rifle hitting the sides of the narrow trench. The messages to expect were 'loose boards', 'hole', 'loose telephone wire', 'head down – snipers', and other similar threats. Some drill on the technique of message passing filched from the excessive bayonet drill exercises would have saved much exasperation and bad temper. It was all a question of timing – instead of the warning being passed the moment when the hazard was reached – it soon speeded up – the warning came in the wrong place and then plonk – foot and leg clad in those damned prehistoric puttees (not the sensible calf length boots of the Germans) were soaked in water. Damned funny for those not caught but no joke when they had to dry out on you.

C.T.s varied in length depending on the contours of the surrounding land. Here it was as flat as a pancake and I suppose this C.T. was half to three quarters of a mile long. Suddenly we were in the front line breastworks and we were welcomed with the greeting 'Not so much bloody noise – Jerry is only a hundred yards away'; actually that is where he was, probably as near as anywhere on the British front, it was just where the breastworks had closed in on a corner. Usually the distance was from two hundred to over three hundred yards.

It was certainly not what I had expected – these breastworks, these artificial trenches, were so different from the seven feet narrow trenches we had been trained in. They were about seven feet high, being built up with the earth filled sandbags with tons of earth deposited on the side facing the Germans so that there was a slope down into No Man's Land at the bottom of which was a belt of barbed wire. Until the tanks came that barbed wire was the greatest protection against a surprise attack and to be caught in only partially destroyed wire was the fate of so many. Behind this barrier was another thick wall of sandbags but built in eight to ten yard blocks with traverses to provide protection from enfilade fire and shell bursts. There was another continuous wall of sandbags behind that in the back of which were 'bivvies' – small recesses supported with timber props where one slept. In this section one could look straight back across the open country and a duck board track ran close to the sandbag wall along this open area.

All this system offered less protection from mortar and shell fire than proper trenches but with the water level only about two feet below the surface breastworks were the only solution. It was ingenious but the constant repair work needed to keep this ramshackle structure intact meant that there was hardly any rest for the front line soldier. In the fire bay was a fire step cut into the sandbags on which one stood at night on sentry-go, head and shoulders above the parapet and looked across the gentle slope into No Man's Land which then sloped up again into the German breastworks which were usually about three hundred yards away. One slept on the firestep when bivvies were flooded.

No Man's Land – I wonder who first gave it that name. How

49

rightly named was that two or three hundred yards which for hundreds of miles separated the great armies. It was a place where no man who wanted to live should ever find himself; a place where one felt absolutely naked and alone and always a place of fear. Fear of noise – the desperate whisperings when the blasted wire would not unroll – the ping of the wire cutter – the tin which one kicked in the dark and the fear of the Very light which brilliantly lit up everything with a ghostly light for a few moments and the tense moment waiting for the dreaded rat-tat-tat of the machine gun. Yes, we really hated No Man's Land.

So this soggy wet bivvy already dripping with water and the fire bay were to be home for the next six days and six nights. It was going to be most unpleasant if the rain continued but the really painful thing for all of us was cold feet – wet cold feet. I had never realised before that cold feet would be the most painful and most wearing of all our discomforts. The ailment named 'Trench Feet' was either frost bite or partial paralysis of muscles and tendons through damp and neglect. This had caused thousands of casualties in the preceding 1915/1916 winter. The ailment was so easy to contract particularly for those who had had enough of the front line. Trench feet was for rankers only as the officers had their waterproof field boots. So for the winter of 1916/1917 a strict anti-trench foot drill was imposed and anyone who managed to get trench feet was to be court martialled. The drill was that each man in each section must take his boots off between 9 a.m. and 10 a.m. but only one man at a time. The dirty feet were to be rubbed with whale oil supplied daily in an old tin. There was no doubt about its being whale oil – no attar of roses was added and after that your feet were a damned sight colder and smellier than before. Except for the few minutes of whale oil application each day boots and socks were worn continuously for the six days up the line; and in my first six days up the line my feet were continuously wet through.

A question I would like to ask historians and romantic writing officers is why these 'patient and cheerful troops', who in 1915/1916 were not conscripts but volunteers, managed to contract trench feet in such large numbers that court martial had to be threatened?

Then there were the rats, the jolly old rats, some black, some brown, and they were very big and fat; may be because in the preceding years food scraps had been thrown away and the rats had flourished and multiplied until they were now almost a plague. In the bivvy any haversack containing food had to be put in the tin hat and be suspended by a string – the alternative was a chewed up haversack, which was the fate of mine on one occasion. With sacking over the bivvy entrance, a lighted candle at night helped to stop them running over you. I always slept with my head in the loose shoulder lining of my overcoat because despite the lighted candle some chaps had been bitten. In this, my first bivvy I had a nice litter squeaking away somewhere amongst the sand bags but I could never find them to dig them out. At night on the firestep any piece of bread or biscuit put beside you on the parapet was quickly snatched away by a dark scuffling shape. It was there – it was gone.

Then there was the other plague, the lice plague, said to cause trench fever; this, however, saved the lives of many of those lucky enough to get it. We were all lousy – the shower bath, clean underclothing and the occasional fumigation of clothing (twice in twenty months for me) was quite ineffective. The first job when getting back to the lousy barns was 'the burning of the seams' in a candle flame.

Was there anything else to grouse about? Yes, the food. This was perhaps the major factor in the feeling of injustice felt by the P.B.I. We were often told that there were seven or eight men behind each man in the front line and rightly or wrongly it was always believed that because we were last in the line the rations had been well and truly got at by the time they reached us. The only time we had a mild mutiny in our battalion was about food. When up the line we always wanted more to eat and much of our shilling a day was spent on food. Rations arrived in the front line in sandbags usually consisting of cold pieces of meat, cold bacon, bread, sugar, tea, and I believe we had some sort of dried or condensed milk. The meat and bacon were quite palatable after the sandbag hairs had been scraped off but we could not understand why our company cooks did not come up to reserve line and give us hot food. We were told that fires could not be made as they might attract shell fire, but what about charcoal fires?

David Jones who wrote that wonderful prose poem 'In Parenthesis' and was in France for the six months December 1915 to early July 1916 writes in his book about the charcoal braziers which were used that winter in the exact few hundred yards of line we now occupied. We saw none of these in the four or five months in the breastworks. What happened to those damned braziers in this winter's tale of 1916/1917? Why, oh why, were they taken away. They would have been an absolute Godsend and it was just as well we did not know about them. Those who did away with their cosy warmth deserve the curses of the frozen P.B.I. For six winter days and winter nights the only way to obtain a hot drink was to use a candle stove, i.e. a tobacco tin in which a shredded candle was placed with a piece of 'four by two' (rifle cleaning flannel – troops for the use of). It took the best part of an hour to make warm tea and I never could get the water to boil. On this narrow bit of No Man's Land with the wind in the right direction the smell of bacon being cooked by Jerry in his front line was the last straw.

I suppose many will say what a tale of woe this is and will it go on and on – what did you expect in the army – a bed of roses? No, in the emotional training period it is difficult to imagine what the stark reality might be, but when you meet it in the filth, mud, and cold of the front line where men lived almost like animals for the routine six days and six nights of winter warfare it is quite a shock. Moreover this is the true, unexaggerated story of the little frustrations apart from the big ones, by which it is hoped to show why the mental attitude of the man in the trench was that of wanting almost at any cost to get away from it. Yet despite everything he carried on, but no credit to him – he damned well had to.

52

After this talk about living standards, what about the fighting? This was winter warfare, just a matter of holding the line before the spring and summer offensives and the war could not be won by the niggling trench mortar strafes, trench raids etc. Each side could have retired a mile or two and saved the pile up of winter casualties and these were considerable. The policy was to keep small operations going, and in the six months ending June 1916 it has been said that over 100,000 casualties were incurred. The French and German practice was more towards live and let live when the big battles were not on. This, however, was not the policy of the Eleventh Army Corps, which was to annoy the enemy as much as possible. Much patrolling with entry to the deserted flooded enemy lines was practised, and the saga of the disastrous holding of posts in the German front line will be described later.

The effect of these operations was one of considerable strain and frustration. I believe that our General Staff were obsessed with the fear that the front line troops would go soft and would not want to fight; that there might be fraternisation such as happened in the Christmas episodes when the Germans and British met in No Man's Land and exchanged gifts. There was possibly something in this because the front line soldier never hated Germans with the hate that was engendered on the home front. We respected each other and even commiserated, saying, 'That old bastard Fritz is probably having as much flooding trouble as we are.'

We had been told that this was a real 'cushy' spot but Divisional Staff knew that and immediately commenced livening things up. In a history of the 56th Division it says that the reputation of this quiet Neuve Chapelle front began to change in October with the opening of the heaviest trench mortar bombardments by the enemy, but there is no question that we started the livening up process. This is indisputable. At all costs the fighting spirit must be maintained, or after a quiet spell the men may not want to fight. Want to fight for King and country, as the phrase goes? After his first six days of dodging Minnenwerfers in the front line not one sane man in a thousand would have refused a return ticket to Blighty.

The exercise of pepping up the fighting spirit was to be commenced at 2 p.m. each day by the daily bombardment of the German front line with Stokes mortars. The three inch Stokes mortar was an ingenious, simple but very effective weapon and consisted of a metal base plate and a long tube about four feet in length. The bomb had a 12 bore sporting cartridge in the bottom which was detonated by a pin in the bottom of the tube when the twenty pound bomb was dropped in. The bomb shot about 150 feet into the air and had a range of 200 to 500 yards. When adjusted for rapid fire forty bombs a minute could be despatched.

A trench mortar team of six men came up next morning and pitched the Stokes outside my bivvy. It was no use my saying, 'Take that bloody thing away from here' – it stayed and at 2 p.m. with a stack of about forty bombs they started. Never did chaps work so hard. The bombs were gone in minutes and I swear they had eight in the air at once. Then it was up with the base plate and tube and down the communication trench in double quick time to their billets behind reserve line, and who can blame them? It took Fritz about an hour to recover from his surprise and then he retaliated mainly with rifle grenades.

We had two casualties, not serious, and for the first time I heard the ominous shout of 'Stretcher bearers'. Stretcher bearers were not Royal Army Medical Corps men; they were never in the line but were always back at the First Field Dressing Stations as often they were not A.I. men and some were conscientious objectors. The stretcher bearers were always two or more men from your own platoon who gave up their rifles and wore white arm bands with a red cross. The first notice of a big offensive was when more stretcher bearers were required and this depleted the number of effective fighters.

The next day Fritz was ready and waiting, and quite soon after the Stokes bombardment he replied with Minnenwerfers or land mines. They were I suppose, some four feet long, weighed nearly 200 pounds (not the Stokes 20 pounds) and they were really terrifying, making a hole almost big enough for a house. At night the glowing fuse could be seen, but in daylight the Minnie was seen as a small dot quickly becoming larger and falling almost vertically with an increasing swish-swish as it turned over.

I was surprised when our corporal, a veteran from early 1916 came round to where I was sheltering in my little bivvy and asked me for the time being to share his. It was obvious to me that he was under a tremendous strain but as a 'rooky' I could not understand why a veteran should react like that, particularly as he was normally such a confident and rather aggressive type. Six months later I knew. After months of strain that is the usual nervous condition of quite sound men. During the early months, although frightened, one can usually conceal it, as one's nerves are not so shattered, but concealment becomes more difficult as times passes. A 'Minnie' hit the breastworks about 150 yards away, killed two, and gave us an all night repair job with Fritz taking pot shots.

I have just used the word 'frightened' and this is a story about frightened men. How can this be when the war memorials carry such inscriptions as 'Our Glorious Dead' – inscriptions so different from Siegfried Sassoon's words, 'the unheroic dead who fed the guns'. So let us stop talking about the glorious dead and think about the frightened living – like the lad who almost crying said to me, 'Why was I ever born' – I wonder why – in less than an hour he had the answer.

I know it will shock some people, particularly parents and relatives who may derive some solace from it, when I say that the almost universal dedication on the Cenotaph and all our war memorials 'Our Glorious Dead' is so untrue. Those dead on the barbed wire of the Somme and in the swamp of Passchendaele did not die gloriously – some died cursing the day they were born. In this war where was the glory – what did their deaths accomplish? – not even a war to end war. If the Versailles Peace Treaty had been one of reconciliation and not revenge they might not have died in vain and there would have been no Hitler, no Belsen, no Hiroshima, and no Dresden. If I had my way I would obliterate the words 'Our Glorious Dead' on every war memorial and in its place inscribe 'We Will Remember Them'.

I know it is not really done – not British – to talk about frightened soldiers. Fear is the last thing anyone wants to admit and in the line, no matter what the circumstances one always tried to avoid being labelled as 'windy'. It is the mental strain of not showing fear that is far more exhausting than fear itself.

When home on leave from the front none of us talked about fear and in deference to the feelings of relatives, friends, and the home front hate atmosphere, understatements and light-hearted references to dramatic and even horrific incidents were the rule. That this attitude was continued after the war can be seen in many of the war stories written by survivors. Except for the occasional one or two per cent we were all windy when in the front line under fire. A man without fear is inhuman – a robot – because fear is a creative human emotion. It is part of the divine spark and only so long as it is part of our make up shall we have humility, love, and normal human attributes. It is surely an essential part of the evolutionary process. In certain circumstances there is nothing wrong in being afraid; what is wrong is in not trying to conquer fear when giving way to it would mean letting down your companions or letting down the side.

It is necessary to write about fear early in this story in order to give some indication of the mental state of men when undergoing nerve shattering shelling and machine-gun fire. That is why the rules of the First World War were so damned unjust and inhuman. Inevitably some men broke down under the constant strain and the noise of the terrific barrages. Nearly three hundred British soldiers were executed for cowardice or desertion and so many of these men were broken by uncontrollable fear. It was so unfair.

Siegfried Sassoon, M.C., refused to fight because he had lost faith in the aims of the war. He was asking the question so often asked by many of us as the war went on and on – what are we fighting for? When involved as the infantry were with face to face killing of the unknown soldier there had to be a better reason for the killing than just to 'beat the Germans'. Sassoon was a wealthy and

The Breastworks

well connected man and a very fine poet and his influential friends managed to have him certified as having some sort of shell shock neurosis. Fifty years later a film was made about this incident. I think he would have been the first to admit that for a private it would have been the firing squad.

On this point I have just read in Guy Chapman's book *Vain Glory* of a case documented by Sylvia Pankhurst. Briefly, in January 1916 a private was blown up by a mine and sent to hospital suffering from wounds and shock. He was soon out of hospital and in February 1916 was back in the line when he wrote to his mother:

> Dear Mother, we were in the trenches and I was ill, so I went out and they took me to prison and I'm in a bit of trouble now and won't get any money for a long time. I will have to go in front of a court. I will try my best to get out of it, so don't worry.

He was duly executed in March 1916, two months after being blown up. Ah well, *c'est la guerre*. The military murders did not happen in the Second World War as there was a better understanding of mental breakdown; in any case it was a very different war – a war of movement, not static siege warfare so lowering to morale, with guns wheel to wheel which lasted for years until the tank provided the key for the breakthrough.

Now to continue with the story. The next day our efficient young officer thought that the best way to avoid casualties might be to get on the duck boards behind the fire bays in a not too compact group and while watching the quickly falling Minnie he would give a signal – one whistle to the right and flatten out in the fire bay, two whistles go to the left and no whistle stay put. This was absolutely nerve-racking, eyes up – looking. We all heard the dull plop when the Minnie was fired and then followed the anxious seconds for the little black dot which so quickly got bigger and bigger with a swish swish swish, then it was run or stay put for your life. This ordeal was waiting for us every afternoon. What you realise, oh so quickly, in the first few days is that you will have to go in and out of the line and sometimes over the top until killed, wounded, or taken

57

prisoner. There was no escape and the Blighty wound, even the loss of a limb was the hope for most of us. 'Lucky bastard' was the usual comment about a man even seriously though not dangerously wounded.

Then there were the mine shafts, another wretched hazard of this area. About every two hundred yards, just behind the breastworks, was a mine shaft where specialist miners were making tunnels underneath No Man's Land and underneath the German trench system. Pumps were hard at it night and day to keep down the water; the miners really earned their money, six shillings a day against our shilling and they looked pretty awful when they came up the shaft, watery eyed and covered with clay. The large Duck Bill crater was quite near where a mine had gone up some months previously. The Germans were, of course, doing the same thing, mining and counter mining, so one never knew whether Kingdom Come was going to materialise underneath you or above you. You really could not win.

The daily life was tough, as the line was so thinly held, there being three or four fire bays between your section and the next. The routine was two hours on sentry go and only two hours off throughout the night instead of the usual two hours on and four hours off, and it was very tiring because during the day work always had to be done on breastwork repairs. This tiredness was quite a big factor in lowering the morale. There was so little rest even when out on 'rest'. The Germans had the French to work for them – the French had their own civilians – the British had only the British army. Talk about bull – every cigarette end and match stick had to be picked up and no waste of any description left about but this belated action was too late to save us from the rat plague. The most favourable time for attack was supposed to be at dawn and again at dusk so throughout the war there was always the routine of 'Stand To' for an hour before dawn and again at dusk when everyone was alerted and gathered in the fire bays.

Dawn was a far from cheerful moment when the frozen huddled up bleary eyed section gathered in the fire bay and with the rubbing of hands and stamping of feet started up the candle stoves for tea. Patient cheerful soldiers! How the hell could anyone be cheerful in such circumstances. Sometimes there was a rum ration, very, very carefully measured out and a dessertspoonful of 40 overproof rum ran through you like fire. It should have been twice as much, twice as often but rightly or wrongly we always said it was so well milked en route that we were lucky to get any at all. Didn't we grouse and grumble. Front line troops were nearly frozen stiff and receiving the thin end of food and rum rations.

Sentry duty at night meant standing on the fire step head and shoulders above the parapet with another man and staring into No Man's Land for two hours until relieved for a two hour rest. There was always a possibility of being hit by a random bullet when Fritz was testing his machine-gun. Apart from that, most nights were fairly quiet. There was, however, much tension when some of our own people were out examining wire etc., because one never knew whether they were Germans creeping about. We were always told the pass word when the patrol went out but notification of return was often forgotten.

It was particularly tense when the Germans decided to have a dark night without putting up Very Lights. These were magnesium flares shot from a heavy pistol to about a hundred feet high which slowly dropped with a very bright light. The strange difference between us and the Germans was that they continuously put up flares while we hardly put up any, so the night when he stopped his flare display was always rather nerve-racking as he was probably out in No Man's Land wiring, wire cutting, or on patrol. We had the edge on him here because he never had any indication of what we were up to . Wiring party, patrol, raid – these words always caused that peculiar sinking feeling for everyone except those few men fortunate in war who had little imagination.

How relevant things are, for after being out in No Man's Land on one of these expeditions the front line seemed a haven of refuge. A wiring party was either (a) a patrol of two or three men to examine our own wire, (b) a party to cut German wire prior to a raid, (c) a

59

repair party of a dozen or more men with iron screw pickets, rolls of wire, or concertinas of made up wire or wired knife rest trestles. The large wiring party effort was always a very windy business. The kicking of a tin, the ping of wire unrolling and the noise made by wire cutters with the Germans only a few yards away was disquieting. The German habit of putting up so many Very Lights was most annoying.

The one thing the experienced man knew and which 'rookies' had to be most emphatically told was that you must stand perfectly still, head on chest. Amongst all the wire and debris of No Man's Land you could not be picked out; the fatal thing was movement. Seton Hutchison in *Warrior* talks of plunging down into the wire and debris when a flare went up. This was quite wrong, but then he was a machine-gunner and the Machine Gun Corps never had anything to do with wiring parties in No Man's Land. In trench warfare they were always in a reserve position some three or four hundred yards behind the infantry where in the 1916/1917 battles and line-holding their function was to give overhead fire like artillery, which they did very effectively. It was when the Germans were on the offensive that the Machine Gun corps bore the brunt of maintaining a position and smashing a German attack, in the same way that in all our offensive battles the German heavy machine-guns, often in concrete emplacements, were the killers. In these situations the heavy machine-gun was a vital weapon and if a position had to be held the gunners had to stick it out with little hope of getting away. This they did magnificently in the 1918 German attacks, particularly in the battle of the Lys at Meteren.

The two hours on and two hours off for six nights was so tiring that on the sixth night all sorts of things could be 'seen' in No Man's Land. The last ten minutes of the two hours seemed a century – time stood still and I am afraid many men nodded off. Our Division had a pioneer battalion which did a lot of heavy labouring and heavy repair work even in the front line breastworks. One section had a very officious officer who tried to throw his weight about with us and was much disliked.

Later, we heard a story that one night while examining the breastworks he found Lewis gun sentries dozing in a fire bay; in fact they had dozed right off, so he picked up the Lewis gun and delivered it to Company H.Q. Sleeping on sentry duty could be a capital offence and with this outside interference the matter could not be hushed up and court martial and executions followed. There was a rumour at a much later date that the officer had been accidentally killed.

At the end of my first six days we came back to the Croix Barbée barn and the relief after Minnie dodging was terrific. As we passed the ruined church of Richbourg I recalled to mind with some emotion at the sight of green grass and hedgerow flowers Wordsworth's line, 'Thoughts that do often lie too deep for tears'. I felt that if I came through the war I would never again grumble about the petty discomforts in civilian life. On this theme, a number of us often said that we would be content with almost anything provided that we were out of danger and had plenty of sleep, food, and plain comforts. How soon one forgets. The one thing uppermost. in my mind after the first six days was why did I join the infantry. Any other branch would have been better. The relief of being in the reserve line some four hundred yards back was enormous. Why, oh why, did I join the P.B.I.?

First of all, we had to have a clean up with a shower bath and clean underclothing, which would however again be lousy within a few hours; so with eager anticipation we marched off and after about a mile we came to the baths. There they were in a field – some baths! It was a corrugated iron compound, almost wide open to the elements and this housed an authentic Heath Robinson or Emmett contraption which consisted of a boiler with the hot water going through a small elevated tank from which the water flowed to pipes having small water can roses at intervals so in groups of twelve we stood shivering underneath those roses and at a signal from the corporal in charge on came the hot water – usually too damned hot and quick was the word as the shower did not last long. The slow ones were left covered with soap and no more water

– a sorry predicament, but damned funny for those not caught.

We were in first reserve which meant that every night we went up to the front line carrying duck boards, hurdles, wire etc. During the day it was bull and more bull, but we could cheerfully stand that because at last we had hot food, bacon, meat stew and tea. Unfortunately just at this time, the marvellous tins of butter became tins of margarine and there was no more butter for the rest of the war.

From a nearby stores dump ran a narrow gauge rail track on which a truck was loaded and pushed to the beginning of the communication trench. Those trucks often became derailed and it was quite a struggle to get them on the rails again. The Germans had a machine-gun trained on this back area and the low buzz of a falling bullet after about a one mile flight was a common noise. One of our Company, a schoolmaster was killed here with an almost spent bullet. He was a fine chap and used to recite poems, including, I remember, 'The Jackdaw of Rheims'.

The six days soon passed and it was up again to the Epinette breastworks. It was cold and very wet. It was a bad week for winter warfare with a number of casualties from the now routine trench mortar strafes and the bivvies were mostly flooded so we had to sleep in the open on the fire step. At last the long six days passed and out we came, tired but looking forward with tremendous zest to six days real rest in a little hamlet called Bout Deville. What a relief with the shadow of death gone for six days. Dramatic, yes, but absolutely true. In the front line you lived constantly with death around the corner. Out of the line you live for the day – the only reality is the present – no past, and certainly no future. What a pity this true philosophy of living did not stay with those who survived the war. Many years later I rediscovered that this was *it* – the only way for a full life.

So spirits rise, and in the farmhouse *estaminets* drinking the crude *vin ordinaire*, usually with citron to take away the sharp tang, or a potent concoction known as Banyules, we have a real carry on. There was no drunkenness and in any case one's funds would not suffice. After paying for eggs and chips and buying candles and food such as the occasional tin of Palethorpe's sausages and always a supply of H.P. sauce to drown the taste of the eternal bully beef, there was not much left for drink out of a shilling per day pay. Shortage of money was a constant trouble and how we envied the Commonwealth troops with five or six times as much.

Most of the meat we had was canned corned beef (bully beef) and although it was of quite good quality it became difficult to eat it continually without sauce. I have never yet been able to understand why this excellent food was so despised. Another item which we really found unpalatable was pork and beans – the pork was half a square inch of fat in the bottom of the tin.

Cigarettes cost just over one franc for a tin of fifty and the usual ration for six days up the line was six tins. Chain smoking was widespread and fifty cigarettes in twenty-four hours was not abnormal. What a solace for frayed nerves. The universal action of front line troops when the bong-zipp-bang whizzbangs got near was to light up cigarettes and nervously puff away wondering whether the next shell would have their name on it. Within seconds they were all at it – those unfrightened men, ready to die gaily.

What absolute rubbish! Given the chance we were always ready to live gaily and this particularly applied to our concert party evenings. The small town of La Gorgue was quite near where the Divisional concert party The Bow Bells gave a most enjoyable show of true professional standard. Talk about drag – there was a chap, I believe, an ex-bugler, who as an alluring dainty flapper was perfect. How the sex-starved troops loved it. Concert party night was one of the highlights of our rest periods. The troupe did a wonderful job, their work was of immeasurable value in raising morale and one could almost forget that the few days of safety would soon be over.

Our billets in this area were always farmhouse barns or outhouses and sometimes there was straw but usually there was just the bare ground to sleep on. What did that matter? We were out of the line and could get a good night's sleep although when the feet got warmed up returning circulation was very irritating. What a nuisance feet were – too cold in the line, too hot out.

Something had to be done to keep up morale and some took to religion, as I did later on, though only for a time. I found poetry helped; I always liked poetry and in one way, I suppose as a somewhat idealist gesture I took my school *Golden Treasury* to France. Actually it became invaluable – it was my talisman – so much so that when a whizzbang blew my haversack and contents to smithereens I was windy for weeks until another *Golden Treasury* arrived from England. Strangely enough the only time this new copy was not with me in the line was in May 1918 and I was gassed! My pack with all my possessions had been left at Battalion H.Q. and although I wrote from the hospital in Scotland I got nothing back – I had so wanted my diary, which I had kept despite orders which forbade the keeping of diaries. The fact that I kept a diary has considerably helped my memory of things past and I rewrote the most outstanding incidents in the summer of 1918.

Much fine poetry was written during the First World War by Wilfred Owen, Siegfried Sassoon, Edmund Blunden and many others, and I wonder why relatively so little came out of the Second World War. To know the truth about war read the poets, not histories and war correspondents' stories; you will find that what I say so inadequately about the pity of war they say with poignant realism. There were many moments of beauty, the nocturne of flickering Very Lights when viewed from a couple of miles back, sometimes seven or eight in the air at once in a clear starlit sky was one such moment. I remember looking at them one night at Croix Barbée and recalling a few lines of poetry seen probably in some magazine which ended with:

A dead man's face is white even at night
And I dry my hands which are trained to kill
And I look at the stars for the stars are beautiful still.

Not great poetry, but in such surroundings it was quite a thought. The following poem by Alan Seeger, written in 1915 has always been in my mind:

Chateau Wood. The desolation at Passchendaele after the battle.

This was home. A Lewis Gun team in front line breastworks

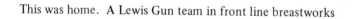

Highway to hell. Passchendaele, 1917

Hellfire corner, now over three miles from the battle front

I have a rendezvous with Death
At some disputed barricade
When Spring comes back with rustling shade
And apple blossoms fill the air –
I have a rendezvous with Death
When Spring brings back blue days and fair.

It may be he shall take my hand
And lead me into his dark land
And close my eyes and quench my breath –
It may be I shall pass him still.
I have a rendezvous with Death
On some scarred slope of battered hill,
When Spring comes round again this year
And the first meadow flowers appear.

God knows 'twere better to be deep
Pillowed in silk and scented gown,
Where love throbs out in blissful sleep,
Pulse nigh to pulse, and breath to breath;
Where hushed awakenings are dear ...
But I've a rendezvous with Death
At midnight in some flaming town,
When Spring trips north again this year,
And I to my pledged word am true,
I shall not fail that rendezvous.

He did not fail that rendezvous – Death took Seeger's hand before the end of that year.

Then there was Rupert Brooke, who did not live long enough to see any fighting and could only present the then popular idealistic view of a soldier dying for his country with his nostalgic poem 'The Soldier'. My favourite lines are not

If I should die, think only this of me;
That there's some corner of a foreign field
That is for ever England.

but:
    And think, this heart, all evil shed away,
    A pulse in the eternal mind, no less
which somehow echo reconciliation and the oneness and unity of all
life and death.

Well, it was soon back to another portion of the line, Duck Bill
crater. This mine had been blown some months before and with
our saps running out to the crater and German saps on the other
side, it was a nervy business guarding those saps, but fortunately I
missed that duty. This was a period of brilliant moonlight nights
and everything was very quiet with no casualties in our company. I
remember that my sand bag bivvy was very wet with water on the
floor and in desperation I used an extra army shirt which I had
scrounged and treasured, for mopping up, but it was still a very
soggy bed. We went back to the little village of Lestrem – not far
behind the line – perhaps three miles and the people were still
living there. Somehow we got friendly with a baker and his wife
who invited us into their house and we had some lovely fruit pies
with their two daughters Albertine and Cécile looking on. They
were very kind and we went back there most nights and then sadly
we said goodbye for it was up the line again. I hope they escaped
before the German 1918 attack which overran this area.
    Within the front allotted to the Brigade we never returned to the
same section of the breastworks. This time we had a section where
on the first night an enthusiastic officer and one man patrol
reported that our wire in No Man's Land was in a shocking state
and inevitably we were booked for that most windy business of all –
wiring parties. This was not to be the usual small party, but about
thirty men were detailed and that afternoon the gloom was thick
enough to cut with a knife and the comments were unprintable. We
were only about three hundred yards from Fritz and with a crowd
like that casualties were an odds on certainty. Barbed wire was I
suppose the most successful of all defensive devices. Barbed wire
and machine-guns were the chief casualty makers and without

barbed wire in front of a trench one felt terribly exposed.

Darkness came and after the routine evening stand to, out we went into No Man's Land with iron screw pickets, coils of barbed wire and wire cutters. Unfortunately we had no concertinas, which were coils of barbed wire about one yard in diameter which pulled out to a length of two or three yards and were much more quickly erected and with less noise. The nerve strain of these parties was almost unbearable.

Well, the inevitable happened; someone tripped and kicked some metal object and Fritz must have heard the noise, so up went the Very Lights and there was a short burst of machine-gun fire. There was a yell and Edwards next to me was hit and collapsed, groaning quite loudly. The stretcher bearers were soon out and for the moment we crawled back to the haven of our front line. Luckily Fritz must have only been suspicious; I suppose the yell was drowned by the sound of firing otherwise we should have had more machine-gun action.

The officer knew that Edwards was a friend of mine; he was unconscious and looked in a pretty bad way with his chest wound, so he asked me if I would like to make up the stretcher party and I eagerly accepted. For one thing I was definitely not keen to rejoin the wiring party on its next trip into No Man's Land. Taking a stretcher case back some two or three miles is a long job. Many times the stretcher had to be lifted out of the C.T. because of tight corners.

When we got to the dressing station we were very well treated by the R.A.M.C. orderlies being served with hot tea and a good lashing of rum. There was no verdict on Edwards except that he looked in a critical state.

On reporting at Company H.Q. about an hour and a half later we found that we had been left half a mess tin full of 40 overproof rum. The rest of the stretcher party were older and seasoned veterans at the drinking game. I was a very inexperienced beginner, an occasional half pint had been my limit. How good it was standing there sipping the fiery stuff in my turn and I soon felt very happy and staggered back to my front line firestep for a sleep – the only place as the bivvies were flooded.

When I was wakened for my two hours turn on sentry duty, I was told that I staggered up, clambered on to the top of the parapet and tried to get into No Man's Land to take on the German army for wounding my friend Edwards. I was of course blind drunk and soon went completely out. The next day I felt half dead, was continually sick and got no sympathy from anyone. The sergeant major was amused when I said that I was not used to heavy drinking.

At the end of the routine six days we went out on rest to a village called Riez Ballieul and for some reason I was picked for Lewis gun instruction. The Lewis gun was a Belgian invention and there were now enough for one to be allotted to each platoon.

It would probably be as well at this point to explain the names given to infantry groupings and give details of the weaponry. The platoon usually consisted of four sections of about six men, each in charge of a corporal or lance corporal and led by a platoon sergeant and a sub-lieutenant. There was a Lewis gun section, a bombing section, a rifle grenade section and a rifle section. Four platoons made a company, A, B, C, or D, in charge of a captain and four companies and H.Q. staff made a battalion commanded by a Lieut. Colonel with a Major second in command.

At full strength a battalion could number 30 officers and 950 other ranks. Four battalions made a Brigade commanded by a Brigadier General and three Brigades constituted a Division commanded by a Major General. Then came the Army Corps commanded by a Lieutenant General consisting of a number of Divisions, and finally a number of Army Corps constituted an Army commanded by a General of which in France we eventually had five. The tally of the weapons for each Division were 24 heavy Vickers machine-guns and with a Lewis gun for each platoon there were 192 Lewis guns. With the average of only two heavy Vickers machine-guns to a battalion, fire power depended very much on the light Lewis machine gun. The Divisional artillery was about 76 guns (54 eighteen pounders, 4 sixty pounders, and 18 4.5 Howitzers). There were also Stoke mortar and heavy mortar batteries.

The Lewis gun section was considered the élite section as it usually had the best bivvies and missed numerous fatigue duties when in the line. Hodges was the corporal of my Lewis gun team and he had a fabulous Primus stove. How I had envied the hot porridge and hot tea which this most favoured Lewis gun team had. I took my training course and was accepted for the Lewis gun team. I stayed with the Lewis gun for the rest of my time in France. The Lewis gun was on the whole a very effective light machine gun as it weighed only twenty nine pounds. Its disadvantages were a high rate of fire – one magazine, 47 rounds in $3\frac{1}{2}$ seconds, and with continuous firing it soon became overheated and liable to stoppages. Also the workings were so exposed that if one fell in the mud with it the gun could for the time being be out of commission.

While on rest we had the news that Sir Douglas Haig, our Commander-in-Chief, was going to inspect us. This meant days of spit and polish and then came the final inspection by our Colonel. I wore glasses – not ordinary glasses but the pince nez type as I disliked the ugly heavy steel framed goggles officially issued.

As the Colonel passed me, he peered into my face and said, 'Can you do without your glasses, my man?'

'Yes, sir,' says I.

Then, peering a little closer and in a voice of thunder he said, 'Have you shaved this morning my man?'

Then, 'nn-no sir,' I stuttered, 'I only shave once a week.'

'Once a week?' he thundered, going a little purple, 'and you are being inspected by your Commander-in-Chief – damn it, man, you are all fluffy – all fluffy. Sergeant Major, take this man's name.'

He took my name but I heard no more about it but for some weeks 'Fluffy' was my name. For my platoon it was the most outstanding incident on a most boring day. Inspected by our Commander in Chief – my foot! After days of bull, we just streaked past Haig with our 140 to the minute parade step and he did not even look at us, let alone inspect us. He stood on the corner of the road engrossed in talking to our Colonel. Could he not have spared just a few minutes to look at the men – many of whom that summer would die in his battles of attrition? Our remarks after those days of spit and polish were unprintable. It was a fine morale raising exercise.

Then the rains came and the next time up the line the front line was flooded and the water was nearly up to our knees. Two feet of muddy water was the general level in the front line. In both the German lines and ours the sand bag walls were collapsing. The rivetting and wire were mixed up with the muddy mass which made repair work very exhausting. It was a terrible week of exposure. Thigh-length gum boots had been issued and at first we thought they were marvellous but we found that after two or three days of continuous wear the insides and socks became wet with condensation. We then had to stuff dry sand bags scrounged from a reserve dump down the leg but could do nothing about the wet socks. We slept curled up on the fire step with our feet out of the water and yet none of us caught a severe cold, pneumonia, bronchitis or anything else; it was most frustrating not to become ill enough to get away.

The reserve positions were not flooded and it would have been a sensible idea to have withdrawn most of the front line men to the drier reserve line as the Germans had done, but as this would have been the reverse of offensive action we had to stay with the flood water. There was no action and there were no casualties in this six days, the only enemy both for us and Fritz being the elements. This was simply punishing the men for the myth of proving that we had a more offensive spirit than the Germans. There was no key position to hold – just flooded fields and ditches.

This was undoubtedly the worst week of exposure to rain we ever had. Despite the cape-cum-groundsheet we were soaked as we had no shelter whatever from the almost continuous rain, but rest assured we were all very cheerful and patient and ... well, you should know by now the rest of that fiction.

After our turn in reserve line, Christmas 1916 was approaching and we had the bad news that we were taking over the front line on December 24th. Worse news, however, followed when we were told that Lewis gun teams only would hold the front line which meant hundreds of yards between each team. The reason was that from 6 p.m. December 24th until midnight December 25th a slow continuous bombardment of the German position was to be made with shells and Stokes mortars.

The reason for this goodwill exercise was that the fraternisation which had occurred between our front line troops and the Germans at previous Christmases must be stopped at all costs. There had been strange happenings, football with the Germans in No Man's Land, exchanges of drinks and cigarettes and shouts of 'Merry Christmas Tommy – merry Christmas Fritz', and of course this would not do as the front line troops might soon forget to hate each other.

Fraternisation could have been stopped, however, without the vindictive Christmas smashing of the German trenches and bivvies. As I have said before, the trouble was that the front line soldiers did not really hate the unknown Germans, in fact in some measure we respected each other. The hate was further back and particularly at home. But war is war – let brotherly love continue – and you must be brainwashed to hate and hate again that unknown human being so that you will have no qualms when perhaps some day you have to open him up with a bayonet. Of course retaliation was feared and by keeping most of the troops in reserve it was thought that heavy casualties would be avoided.

We went up in the afternoon, a miserable afternoon of heavy cold sleety rain. Luckily we had a fine semi-circular iron bivvy – the first I had seen. It was quite dry and with the Primus stove things could be quite good if Fritz did not retaliate. At 6 p.m. the Stokes mortars started putting over their bombs every half hour and the eighteen pounders joined in. There was no reply from Fritz and no Very Lights for the simple reason that he had left his front line to celebrate Christmas in the good old German manner. We could see bonfires burning two miles back over the flat country. Christmas

Day dawned but still not a whisper from Fritz and our mortars were making a sorry mess of his breastworks. It was weird, there was no other word for it and the slow vindictive Christmas cheer went on all day until midnight. We came out of the line after the routine six days and still no retaliation. This time we were in reserve in Bout Deville village and some days came up the line to repair sagging breastworks.

On New Year's Day, we were just passing the last inhabited farm when it started and for two hours Fritz threw everything he had at our breastworks and on the back areas which were not usually shelled. We dashed for the cellar in the farm and with the frightened farmer and his family we waited for the strafe to quieten down. Then we went up to do our job and what a mess the front line breastworks were in. There had been quite a number of casualties. Only if one believed that attrition would win the war, was there the slightest reason for the childish but fatal game of the Christmas hate and the German New year retaliation.

This time we were billetted in Estaires, a sizeable small town where we were put up in a loft with cows on the ground floor at one end and with us upstairs, it made quite an interesting but rather smelly situation! Then we had our belated Christmas dinner which was held in some sort of a village hall. We let ourselves go with much more zest than we could ever have worked up in civilian life. If war correspondents had been present, they could have truthfully reported that it would have been hard to find a more carefree happier company of soldiers. We were living for the day and to the limit. What a night – there was plenty of hot rum punch and beer and I am always reminded of that night when I hear the song 'My Ain Folk' which our dour Scot sang in his fine baritone voice. He did not survive.

CHAPTER 6

The Saga of the Posts

There had been heavy rain during this rest period and then came the great freeze up. Twenty degrees of frost was the average temperature during the next three weeks and it was said to be the longest cold spell of such severity since 1880. In canteens barrels of beer froze solid and burst, while up the line even the water in the water bottles used as pillows, froze. All this, first the flooding and then the terrific cold led to one of the most senseless, punishing and ineffective exercises that can be imagined.

The extreme weather had caused the partial collapse of the German front line breastworks as it had done to ours, so very sensibly they evacuated the front line and retired four or five hundred yards down their communication trenches to the more comfortable reserve line. With the cessation of the nightly Very Light display a patrol had discovered and reported this retirement. I can just imagine some Staff wallah saying, 'Here's a chance to show the Boche our fighting spirit and a fine challenging exercise for the men; let us establish advance posts in the German front line.'

What a nice simple job for the P.B.I. and another instance of the disregard of casualties which was a feature of the First World War – not the Second. Montgomery and generals like him did all they could to minimise casualties, so this is another episode which is severely critical of the Divisional and Army Corps staff. Obviously these men were doing their damndest to win the war, they were intelligent well trained soldiers, but they were too detached and had only an academic knowledge of the front line conditions. Of course these staff officers were not cowards, but as I have said before there was something wrong with the whole system of communication between the various ranks.

Here then is a detailed account, or rather two accounts, of the Saga of the Front Line Posts. Saga is the word which could be the official description of the exercise – the words used by the P.B.I. involved in it would be 'Operation – Bloody Senseless'. It is reported in detail at great length as a typical example, of the difference between official accounts and actuality, and what a difference! In this area No Man's Land was about 350 yards wide. It was flat and had a thin covering of frozen snow. The posts were possibly some 600 yards apart and set in the parapet of the deserted German front line breastworks so that one looked down into the front line trench. The reserve line to which the Germans had withdrawn some 400 yards back was adequately connected with the front line by communication trenches. During the daytime these small isolated posts were completely cut off from our front line. No one could ever cross the 350 yards of white frozen ground because the German snipers and machine gunners had every inch of it covered. A shot was the reply to any observed movement in our post.

Our post was named Barnet, and to the north was Bertha, to the south Flame and Enfield and the other two posts were called Hampstead Heath and Irma. It was quite obvious to us and it should have been obvious to General Staff that these posts could hardly have been more vulnerable. The Germans had only to proceed in the cover of their communication trenches, surround the posts and kill or capture the occupants. From 9th January to 28th January when the posts were finally given up, German raids were frequent and casualties mounted with practically no loss to the enemy.

Major Dudley Ward, D.S.O., M.C., wrote a book entitled *The 56th Division* and in this he gives a fairly full account of this episode in the usual factual impersonal style of official reports which shows clearly the difference between the mental attitude of the Staff and that of the expendable units involved. The following are extracts from his book:

> The operations of the winter are in fact only of interest as showing the endurance, determination and the spirit of the 56th Division ... There was nothing in the nature of an attack of any magnitude – it was a matter of small parties of men resisting the fearful conditions of climate and penetrating with great boldness into the enemy lines.

Then follows an account of the establishment of posts on the old German front line and how these posts were violently attacked in turn, some more than once. He writes:

> On the 14th a post known as Hampstead Heath was violently attacked by the enemy in very superior numbers. This post was held by the 7th Middlesex and the men were so cold they could scarcely move; The Queen's Westminster Rifles were actually half way across No Man's Land to relieve them when the attack occurred. This relief was driven back by trench mortar barrage and machine-gun attack. The 7th Middlesex put up a fight but their Lewis gun was jammed and useless and they were forced out of the post. On the morning of the 15th January another post called Bertha was attacked under the cover of dense fog and after four men out of eleven were killed the post was driven out but two were taken prisoner. Almost immediately a patrol of the same regiment composed of four men left our front line and reoccupied the post and by noon our troops had restored the position. From the 17th to the 20th the posts were bombarded by artillery and trench mortars and on the 21st under cover of an intense bombardment the enemy succeeded in occupying Bertha Post. In the early morning our patrols discovered the enemy leaving it and it was again occupied...
> The artillery fire which the men had to face was remarkably

accurate and very fierce, and there was also the weather. At first
No Man's Land was a swamp or a lake and then a cold snap set
in which was paralysing to all who had to live in the open. The
men had no cover either from shell fire or the weather – the
'posts' were only a matter of shell holes on our side of the
German breastworks and improved with the help of a shovel and
a pick. In face of these hardships the courage and determination
of the troops of the 56th Division never faltered although at one
time Capt. Newnham felt impelled to write that, 'Although
wiring had been much strengthened actual consolidation is
impossible owing to the frozen ground. The garrison feel they are
occupying shell traps. Battalions are on the defensive and not
offensive and the morale of the men is suffering. At the same time
our existing defences are falling into disrepair.' In spite of this
dictum the men succeeded after it was written in driving off four
severe attacks but it gives an indication of the desperate
conditions under which the 56th Division carried out an
aggressive policy.

All I can say concerning this praise about the occupation and
reoccupation is that we who were doing the occupying and
reoccupying knew that the Germans were laughing at us as they
were never driven out of the posts, but left them for us to reoccupy
ready for their next raid. I was out on Barnet post for two daylight
periods, 7.30 a.m. to 4.30 p.m. and one night period from 4.30 p.m.
to 7.30 a.m. The Lewis gunners were unlucky as with six day shifts
and six night shifts and only four guns to a Company it meant three
times out on the post instead of one; the following is my account of
this exercise.

Just before dawn the Lewis gun team with three other men and a
corporal – a party of ten, went out to relieve the night party of
about twenty men and a sergeant. These posts were always in
charge of a corporal by day and a sergeant by night – no officer
manned the post. We crossed the 350 yards in darkness and just sat
or lay down in the shallow trench for the rest of the day in a

temperature of about 12 degrees Fahrenheit. The ground was rock-hard, and it was impossible to dig a deeper trench, so in daytime we all had to crawl to the improvised latrine because the Germans from their reserve line 400 yards away could see every movement.

Communication with our front line was by a land line telephone, but on both days I was out the line was broken within an hour by the trench mortars which the Germans put over during the day. These were not right on the post but round it because of course they could have wiped us out in a few minutes and they knew that. I agree with the official account that the fire was accurate – not right on the post but all round it, as they wanted us to stay and be easy meat for their night raid. What about morale when trapped in a senseless exploit of this kind? We were just sitting ducks.

It soon became light and Fritz started with his morning strafe. One shell pitched fairly near and a splinter hit one of the chaps on the ankle; it was a bit of a mess but the bleeding was not excessive, we dressed it and he lay there all day. We could just pick out Flame post some 600 yards to our right and had seen a moving black shape on the white ground of what must have been a wounded man. The Germans were taking pot shots and with less than a hundred yards to go he was hit again. A few minutes later stretcher bearers pulled him in and Fritz did not fire on them.

After that episode our own casualty wisely decided to freeze up and wait until it was dark and the cold soon stopped most of the pain. I remember the pain of cold feet and legs and then the numbness as the long day wore on. When darkness came and the night party arrived it was quite difficult to stagger across the 350 yards of No Man's Land and we still had to stay in the front line in the freezing temperature and no hot food was supplied.

This was a terribly windy period, especially as there were two more stints to do. Fritz frequently successfully raided these posts, killed some men and took prisoners; one night it would be Barnet post and our worry was whose turn would it be to be out there. The Germans were so confident that they rather advertised the raid as a few gas grenades were put over about 4.30 p.m. when the Lewis

77

gun team, bombing section and the sergeant went out.

Then about 8 p.m. one of the sentries on the perimeter of the barbed wire said that he saw the glow of cigarettes in the deserted front line trench and heard very quiet noises which might be someone crawling about and not rats. The tension of listening and waiting as the Germans commenced to surround the post was nerveracking for everyone in the post.

The planned defence against a raid was to have a platoon always at stand to in the front line and there was a Stokes mortar battery always ready to put a barrage round the post immediately the S.O.S. rocket went up. On hearing about the glowing cigarettes the sergeant immediately sent back for the stand-to troops to rush out and then lit the S.O.S. rocket which luckily fizzled and did not go off. If it had gone off the Germans would probably have rushed the post. As it was, the German box barrage of shells which crashed down to isolate the post from the front line, missed the stand-to troops by seconds and they were in the post.

Then there were a few minutes of mad inferno, of bombs, rifle fire, Lewis gun fire and above all the noise a German shout of 'English Vipers' which was a very strange description of us. A London cockney, a fine soldier, but with little imagination and almost fearless, was pulling out the pins of the Mills bombs and with the fuse burning was tossing them to the bombing corporal who had the best throw in the platoon. It would have been Kingdom Come for one or two if this unique bombing exercise had misfired.

The Lewis gun was rushed out to a small mound to get a better field of fire but the flame from the gun immediately brought a shower of egg bombs which knocked out the corporal and No. 1. One of our best singers was killed and the whole abortive raid was over in a matter of minutes.

It was about the first time a post had been held and the incident was mentioned in the British war communiqué of the day and appeared in the British press viz: 'One of our advanced posts east of Fauquisart was raided but the raiders were beaten off with heavy loss.'

I do not know about heavy loss, there were no German bodies to be seen next day, only a couple of blood stained overcoats. I believe there was a medal for the Company Commander who organised the successful defence, but it was the alert sentry and the quick decision of the sergeant which saved the post.

I was out on the post again on the last day for another freeze up of the limbs. When we left at 4.30 p.m. in the evening darkness, H.Q. buglers had been sent up to help us back across No Man's Land and down the communication trench where there was an ambulance waiting. Yes – an ambulance to transport unwounded front line soldiers. We were in the front line for the whole six days and even apart from the three periods on the post the exposure in that temperature was almost killing. We were told that one man actually died from exposure on one post when his relief was overlooked. After three weeks of post holding, something of the plight of the P.B.I. must have at last percolated to Army H.Q. because the posts were given up on this last day – the 28th January by the order of the Army Commander General Horne.

Lieutenant General Haking showed his appreciation by sending the following letter to Major General Hull, 56th Division:

Corps Commander to General Hull:
I should be glad if you would convey to the troops of the division under your command my appreciation of the operation they have carried out so successfully during the last month in establishing posts in the German front line and holding them in spite of heavy bombardments and hostile infantry attacks.

The effects of the operations are much greater than the troops that took part in them are probably aware of; they have shown the enemy the offensive and enterprising spirit displayed by our troops and have encouraged other British formations to adopt similar tactics which will have a far reaching effect.

Brig-Gens. Loch and Freeth who conducted the operations at different periods when you were acting in command of the Corps deserve credit for the determined manner in which they continued the pressure against the enemy in spite of serious opposition. The various counter attacks by our troops immediately delivered without waiting for any further orders and simply adhering to the plan laid down by you show a fine military spirit on the part of the officers and men of the battalions engaged.

I was particularly pleased with the action of the scouts of the 1st London Regt. who went across No Man's Land in daylight on the 14th January, and with the prompt action of 'B' Company Queen Victoria's Rifles under Capt. Brand, on the night of January 22nd/23rd when the posts were attacked. Also with 'A' and 'B' Companies of the London Rifle Brigade, under Lieut. Prior and 2/Lieut. Rose, who held Enfield and Barnet posts in the enemy line on the night of January 24/25th, when their posts were shelled with lachrymatory shells and our men had to wear respirators. These posts were then heavily attacked, and the supporting platoons quickly traversed No Man's Land before the hostile barrage was put down. I am also glad that the artillery support on all occasions throughout these operations has been prompt and effective.

R. HAKING, Lieutenant General,
Commanding XI Corps.

3rd February 1917.

So there we were – congratulations all round. This letter presents such a fictitious picture of the operation that it must be analysed in some detail as it is so typical of the eye wash contained in many official reports of operations. General Haking's knowledge came via the long line of communication – Battalion – Brigade – Division – Army Corps and it is possible that he thought he had a reasonably true picture. I must reiterate that this is the typical glossy account which appeared in the communication network.

Everyone can now read how General Charteris, the great optimist, Chief of Intelligence, fed Haig with picturesque stories of victories which were bloody failures particularly in the

Passchendaele battle. Again, why should Lieutenant General Sir
Lancelot Kiggel, Haig's Chief of Staff, have been so ignorant of the
Passchendaele swamp that he broke down when he saw it? It is said
that General Kiggel only saw a battlefield once – very long after the
battle. The truth is that the back room boys known by the common
soldier as the Brass Hats knew very little about front line
conditions. Now for a critical examination of the Haking letter
phrase by phrase to corroborate these remarks:
(a) 'my appreciation of the operation carried out so successfully'.

The operation of occupying a deserted German line without
opposition was no great feat and the holding of the posts was a
dismal failure, many men being killed and taken prisoner by the
Germans with no loss to themselves.
(b) ...'holding them in spite of heavy bombardments and hostile
infantry attacks'.

These posts could not have been held more than a few minutes if
the Germans really wanted us out. Their trench mortars could
easily have obliterated them. In daylight the posts were completely
cut off and the hostile infantry attacks were the night raids which
were all successful except the raid on our post.
(c) 'The effects ... are much greater than the troops that took part
in them are probably aware of ... and have encouraged other
British formations to adopt similar tactics.'

Was Haking told that literally frozen stiff, we had to be helped
back across No Man's Land with an ambulance waiting at the end
of the communication trench? If similar tactics were adopted
elsewhere someone needed a brain examination.
(d) 'Brig. Gens Lock and Freeth who conducted operations ...
deserve credit for the determined manner in which they continued
pressure against the enemy in spite of serious opposition. The
various counter attacks by our troops immediately delivered ...'
The pressure exerted by the Brigadiers from some miles back was
not against serious opposition. The Germans after raiding the posts
could always have stayed in possession in their own front line with
their communication trenches running up to it, if they had wanted

to. After the successful raids they left them for reoccupation by the sitting ducks without fighting. There were no counter attacks to drive the Germans out.

(e) The Lieutenants mentioned did excellent work in getting the platoons across No Man's Land but the posts were always in charge of a sergeant by night and a corporal by day.

This operation has been dealt with at some length as it is probably rare for a participant to have such intimate knowledge and then some day to be able to read the official report on it. It was not worth one of the many men's lives so wantonly sacrificed. It was just one hell of a week all for nothing and our morale was as low as low could be with exasperation and frustration at being treated as expendable units. Can anyone wonder at the changed attitude of the P.B.I. when faced with so much indifference to casualties and hardships?

It is quite likely that critics will say this writer does nothing but grouse; thank God that for the war effort we had men of a different calibre. Different calibre? Men of my thinking did their job and did not let the side down, but of course we criticised, of course we were sick of our participation in this kind of war fought in this kind of way, the object of which was getting more obscure every day. This exploitation of a man's sense of loyalty and patriotism, this exploitation of a volunteer's almost ingrained sense of *esprit de corps* would not be forgotten or forgiven by anyone who had to endure this fatal fantastic piece of nonsense played out in a temperature of 12 degrees F.

It is rather strange but I once had a very short parley – monosyllabic – with this same General Haking in the Neuve Chapelle area a few weeks after my front line baptism. I well remember General Haking inspecting our battalion in the driest part of a rather muddy field and I suppose because I looked rather young and was not a very large soldier he stopped in front of me – the whole retinue of red banded Staff officers stopped – the Colonel and his retinue stopped and I wondered why.

Then the General said, 'Well my boy, things are not really as bad as they say they are – are they?' and to this loaded question to my lasting regret I stuttered 'N-no sir', despite the fact that I had just had a shattering week of 'Minnie' dodging. If I had spoken the truth I should have said, 'They are much worse – it's bloody awful.' Apart from not having the nerve and with the Colonel and top brass looking on how could I let the battalion down?

This small incident illustrates a most important point. When Generals, Commanding Officers and such like question the men about conditions, or even if there are no complaints, why should it be thought that the men are content and have nothing to grouse about. On this point *General Jack's Diary: 1914-1918*[1] has an entry 'The men are great-hearted fellows. Their legs, capes and jerkins are habitually soddened with wet clay ... In spite of extremely long hours on duty in great discomfort, hard labour repairing the parapets and other defences, besides no proper meals in the trenches, there is little grumbling and never a whine ...' Did he really expect the men to whine? I can just see the Colonel and the Battalion Sergeant Major congratulating the man who whined. His life would have been Hell, so the often false picture of high morale and contented troops was maintained.

There was a large increase of air activity in the early months of 1917. On our front a character known as the Mad Major did a lot of low flying and the sky was dotted with the black smoke of German archies, as anti air craft shells were called. Our shells burst with white smoke. Air battles were fascinating to watch as they took place at relatively low altitudes and sometimes the pilots could be seen in the open cockpits. The rat-tat-tat of the Lewis gun being fired up in the sky was easily recognisable and was the signal that a scrap was on. Our planes used the Lewis gun with a double magazine of 97 rounds instead of the normal 47 and then came the newly invented synchronised mechanism which allowed firing straight ahead through the propeller which revolutionised air fighting.

[1] Edited by John Terraine: Eyre & Spottiswoode, 1964.

For some days we saw the Richthofen circus in action; they monopolised the air space for a time and we were able to pick out the Baron's red plane. Our rest billet at this time was in a racing stable at Laventie. The spire of the church was still balanced and pitted and another memory is that of the incongruous site of an eighteen pounder gun in the overgrown garden of a villa on the outskirts of Laventie. Tennant's poem 'Home Thoughts in Laventie' is very nostalgic. The first verse is

> Green gardens in Laventie!
> Soldiers only know the street
> Where the mud is churned and splashed about
> By battle-wending feet;
> And yet beside one stricken house there is a glimpse of grass,
> Look for it when you pass.

I always remember the relief of seeing the green grass after the mud of the trenches. Tennant was killed in 1916 aged 21; what he might have written! Consider what we lost: Butterworth aged 31, killed in 1916, and we are left with so little of his beautiful music –'The Shropshire Lad Rhapsody', the Songs, and 'Banks of Green Willow'. Then there was Wilfred Owen killed November 1918, Alan Seeger killed 1916, Edward Thomas killed at Vimy 1917 and many others who had so much to give while so many of us who survived had so little. Wilfred Gibson's moving poem written, I believe, after the war 'The Golden Room' contains the sad lines about Thomas (who was in the gathering of Georgian poets on that still summer evening in July 1914):

> Thomas lies
> 'Neath Vimy Ridge where he, among his fellows
> Died, just as life had touched his lips to song.

What a gamble survival was.

The routine winter programme went on – in and out of the line with not many casualties. Then there was some excitement with the arrival of the Portuguese who were to take over our section of the line. Poor devils – what on earth had they to fight for? But they were our allies so the Portuguese government sent their lads to fight in our war. They held this section until May 1918 when the Germans walked through them in the Merville attack. The obvious nickname for them was 'Pork and Beans' but there was quite a row about it and in battalion orders we had the strict instruction that the practice must cease forthwith – our allies must not be called pork and beans, but of course after that there was no hope of the practice ceasing. They were regulars and appeared quite smart and efficient. Just at this time there was an even stranger ally – a Chinese labour force which we saw working on the roads in the rear area.

CHAPTER 7

Arras 1917

On March 1st 1917 we left the Laventie area for good and started our long march for the long promised rest. We marched four days covering about twelve miles a day through unspoilt country with clean barns to sleep in and sometimes straw to sleep on. How peaceful everything was with no sign of war and spring just around the corner. Cheerful troops? You bet we were cheerful, we were out for a long rest and determined to make the most of it. Any war correspondents seeing us miles behind the line in this mood would naturally write about cheerful troops and high morale, but it would have been a different story if they had seen us in those soggy breastworks and flooded trenches.

The Lewis gunners had a two wheeled cart into which was loaded the gun, spare parts, panniers of ammunition, our packs and often the sergeant major's pack. The cart was dragged along by ropes, three men on each side and it was easy in the flat country, but oh the difference in undulating country; we could never keep up with the company and usually arrived at the night's billet half an hour late.

On the fourth night the rumour that the Germans had retreated from their front lines caused considerable excitement. How we longed for the end of the war and any rumour which might save our lives was eagerly listened to, but later we heard that they had only fallen back to a strongly fortified trench system known as the Hindenburg Line.

I doubt whether it would have been possible to find a more fed

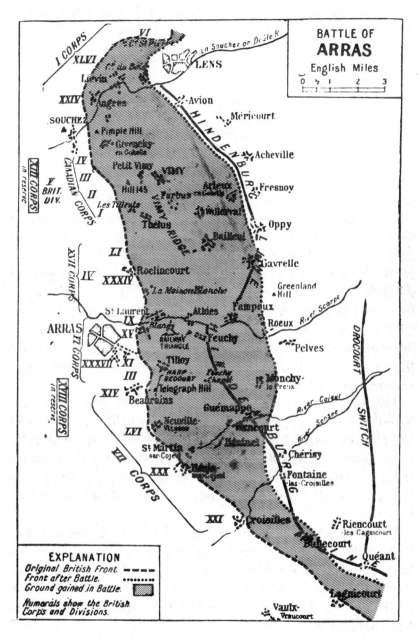

I CORPS

VI

L'C St Dalle

La Souchez or Deûle R.

LENS

XLVI

F'e du Bois

Lievin

Avion

XXIV

Angres

Méricourt

SOUCHEZ

Pimple Hill

Acheville

Givenchy
en Gohels

IV

Petit Vimy

VIMY

Fresnoy

III

Hill 145

Acheux

II

Farbus extension

Givenchal

Les Tilleuls

I

Oppy

Thelus

Bailleul

Gavrelle

LI

Greenland
Hill

IV

XXXIV

Roclincourt

La MaisonBlanche

Fampoux

St Laurent

Athies

IX

Roeux

River Scarpe

ARRAS

XV

Feuchy

Pelves

Blangy

Railway
TRIANGLE

XXXVII

XI

Tilloy

Monchy-
le-Preux

III

Chapel
RODOAR

Feuchy
Chapel

XIV

Telegraph Hill

Beaurains

Guemappe

LVI

Neuville-
Vitasse

Wancourt

St Martin
sur-Cojeul

Mæsnil

Chérisy

XXX

Fontaine
les-Croisilles

DROCOURT SWITCH

HINDENBURG

RIDGE

River Cojeul

River Sensée

XXI

Croisilles

Riencourt
les-Cagnicourt

Bullecourt

Quéant

VII CORPS

Cagnicourt

Vaulx-
Vraucourt

CANADIAN CORPS

V
BRIT.
DIV.

XVII CORPS

EXPLANATION
Original British Front - - - -
Front after Battle. ••••••••
Ground gained in Battle. ▨
Numerals show the British
Corps and Divisions.

The Areas fought over in the Battles of Arras 1917 and 1918

87

up, browned off lot of troops when next morning we were told that we must immediately carry on marching – not for the promised rest but back to the line at Arras. Cheerful troops? What a sell-out. Another grouse, but surely there was some reason for it. This meant another five days' marching when we should have completed a neat 120 miles semicircle. Nine days continuous foot slogging was very tough and ambulances were on hand for the fall outs. The Lewis gun team however kept going, in fact I never fell out of any march; possibly my fairly light weight of 10½ stones was about right for tests of endurance.

A few days later after marching for miles along the screened main road we reached Arras and its cellars. Arras was a deserted town and there were no civilians, no eggs and chips, no wine, just army canteens, Y.M.C.A. and Church Army huts in which to spend our pay; how we missed the French *estaminets* of Flanders – it was a different world.

The German retreat had completely upset the plans for the spring offensive as the caves just outside Arras, with light railway tracks, roads and accommodation for thousands of troops had been greatly enlarged for the battle. Long tunnels had been made linking up these caves. There were two main tunnels (a) the Ronville tunnel which went south to south east to Beaurains and was now of little use, and (b) the St. Saveur tunnel which went more to the east to Tillois and was still very useful. There was accommodation in these caves and tunnels for about twenty thousand men. Of course had we known of the German withdrawal plan much unnecessary work could have been saved.

For some days we were hard at work carrying ammunition, bombs, and general supplies to our new front positions and it was a strange feeling walking over the old German trenches. At this point, they had gone back only about a mile and a half to Vimy Ridge. Our new temporary front line was an old German communication trench and to reach it we had to go through the main street of the ruined village of Beaurains. It soon had a new name – death village. On the way up, being loaded with supplies you just prayed, but on the way back everyone just ran like hell down that ruined main street. The Germans had a battery of whizzbangs trained on the street and fired salvos when parties were going through. There were a number of casualties but our company escaped very lightly. Later we heard the rumour that four Germans were found in a cellar and that they signalled to a battery every time a party went through the village. The nerve strain of running the gauntlet each night was pretty awful.

As the German retreat had upset the original Spring offensive plan, some rethinking was necessary. The main allied offensive was to be the much heralded Nivelle attack by the French across the River Oise and Aisne, to be preceded by the British Arras attack a few days before in order to create a pincer movement breakthrough.

Little, however, was known of the formidable Hindenburg Line defence system. The Canadians had been given the key task of capturing Vimy Ridge which so often had proved the graveyard of previous offensives. It was a tremendous task, but they had had excellent training and every man had seen maps and models. Above all, there was ample communication between all ranks.

The tempo was building up for the big push and the batteries of guns wheel to wheel along the Tillois road were most impressive. Then there was the cavalry, which we saw in the back area. We thought it was a tremendous gamble to think of using cavalry against barbed wire protected trenches with machine-gun nests strategically placed; yet on the first night after the attack there was a two mile gap in the German defence system which the cavalry might have exploited, but the moment passed, as they had been held too far back. When they actually came into the forward area German spotter planes soon put paid to the cavalry idea as they were soon observed and decimated with shrapnel. The dead horses were lying about for weeks as just under the sub soil was hard chalk rock and they could not be buried. This chalk made it almost impossible to dig jumping-off trenches for the attack, which was unfortunate as we were a long way from the new German line underneath the prominent ridge.

During this waiting period we were in the old German communication trench and there was no shelter of any kind. The heavy shelling on both sides rose to a crescendo and the whole ridge in front seemed to be going up in smoke. It was the most intensive shelling I had so far seen. Unfortunately the heavy counter shelling by the Germans on the Arras – Beaurains road cut off our supplies and we had no water or food for two days. It was the first time I had experienced such a terrible thirst and I remember that when a heavy shower of rain filled footmarks in the muddy trench bottom, we scooped up the water and drank it with no ill effects.

At last water and rations arrived, but the water was in new petrol tins not washed out and being also chlorinated it was almost undrinkable. This was a very miserable few days because the bottom of the trench had no duck boards and the frequent rain showers turned it into a mud morass, so much so that one chap in extracting his leg left his boot buried in the mud.

The Germans were some distance away and we could not see any trench system. Of course they knew all about the impending attack and effectively stopped us putting out daylight scouts by heavy machine-gun fire. Machine guns were more feared than shells and the German heavy machine gun was the main killer in all attacks. If one lasts long enough one gets an expert knowledge of the sounds of warfare and this knowledge is often a life saver. One hears the rat-tit-tat of machine gun as it traverses towards you and then there is the rising note until when right on you it becomes a vicious crack-crack-crack. It is similar to isolated shell fire; one soon recognises the lower whine of the shell which will pitch a hundred yards away, but the tremendous split second shriek of the same calibre shell which will pitch within a few yards is ever after remembered.

On the point of sounds in warfare we always said that, when standing on the fire step on the Neuve Chapelle front with its three hundred yards of No Man's Land, if you heard the crack of the German rifle you were okay because you would never hear the sound of the bullet which killed you. This reminds me of an incident in this area when we had just come into the line with new sand bag material covers on our tin hats in order to make German Intelligence think that another Division had taken over. I was on the fire step on the first night with the usual desultory rifle fire coming across, when suddenly there was a shout from the fire bay a few yards away and in rushed a young lad – a chap known to have little imagination and no fear, holding out his tin hat.

He said, 'Just look what the bloody bastards have done to my new cover.'

We looked – a bullet had cut a clean furrow through the side of his tin hat about a quarter of an inch from his head, and that was his reaction. It was no pose, Fritz had had the damned cheek to muck up his new cover. How we laughed.

We came out from the mud heap on my twentieth birthday and went back a few miles to Bienvillers for a short rest. During this period the air fighting was intense and much of it took place in full view a thousand or so feet up. With planes flying at only about 160 miles an hour we had a grandstand view but unfortunately we saw many of our fast climbing new tri-planes shot down. The British air losses during this period were very heavy. Then finally we appeared to gain the air mastery so necessary for the impending attack. We always had plenty of notice of a stunt because more stretcher bearers were selected from our ranks, but in the big attack the stretcher position is often pretty hopeless because after a few casualties the stretcher bearers are gone for hours. If the attack is successful the wounded are lucky and can be picked up, but if it fails the badly wounded are left in No Man's Land often with no help.

The weather changed and became very cold and then we went to the cold damp caves to prepare for the Easter Monday 9th April 1917 attack on Neuville Vitasse which was at the southern flatter end of Vimy Ridge. Then I had a big slice of luck and was told to pack up and go back some miles for a course at a Lewis gun school; so I missed the attack. The school was in unspoilt country and it was wonderful to be away from the line. It was spring, it was all sunshine, with time to think – there was plenty to think about.

Freedom to think was the one great asset in this army life. Physically you had no freedom – you did as you were told with no argument – your food, clothes and lodgings were provided with no question of alternatives, and this left you mentally free with much more freedom than could ever be achieved in civilian life. When out of the line and amongst the trees, grass, and wild life of the countryside there was a great affinity with nature, reminiscent of the times when during school holidays I would get up very early and walk up Nightingale Valley, the valley underneath Clifton Suspension bridge to a small clearing in Leigh woods and sit on a tree trunk and look at things. In the words of Davies, when on these courses and away from the line there was again 'time to stand and stare'. Many other soldiers have written about this phenomenon of mental freedom which army life gave.

However the holiday was soon over and it was back to the battalion, who were out on rest after a reasonably successful 'over the top', when the Canadians captured Vimy Ridge and our Division captured Neuville Vitasse and Wancourt. They had not suffered too badly.

In the Nissen hut camp at Bienvillers it was fine to meet the old team again; Morton, however, was missing, but he was found seven days later in No Man's Land, still alive and I think he survived. So far I have hardly mentioned my companions, however, my close friend was No 1 on the gun, a tall fresh faced Londoner named Simpson. By this time we both now had the same cynical outlook about the war and like most others were feeling the strain and we talked quite a lot on serious matters, trying to find out what there was in life for us, if anything. I wonder why both of us suddenly decided to take a serious interest in religion, and yet on reflection there was not much need to wonder. In the main it must have been fear. The odds were surely against us in this life, so why not try to book a place in the next. Too cynical? Possibly – after all at the age of twenty the young often have a phase of religious fervour. After my intensive religious education – often twice to church on Sunday, plus afternoon Sunday school class, it was easy to return. One of my best subjects was religion and I had won school prizes for biblical knowledge, but all this could not have struck very deeply as I so easily gave up church going when I started work in London.

The outcome of our discussion was that we had a long talk with the padre and decided to take a full part in the Church of England work in the battalion i.e. helping in the work of maintaining the temporary churches we made in tents and barns, and in forming discussion groups.

Our padre was High Church, tall, handsome, completely fearless and he often went over with the troops in an attack. He had already been awarded the Military Cross. He used to hold communion services in full regalia in the reserve trenches before an attack. He was an admirable type and yet one could never get very near him as there was always a certain detachment, possibly a barrier he could not help. His sermons on the compulsory church parades were full of the usual platitudes. How could it be otherwise? I think the position of the padre was almost impossible – it was compromise, compromise, compromise. By this time, when on parade, the troops were often told by their commanders that 'the only good German is a dead one – kill the Boche – we don't want prisoners' and the padre on the Sunday church parade was expected to preach a Christian sermon on 'do unto others' etc., 'and love your enemies'. It could not, of course, be done, but at this period for me the penny had not dropped. The clear glass of reason was misted up by obsession with my own salvation. The outcome of this religious revival both for Simpson and myself was that our world was a better place to live in, but this lasted for only about three months until Passchendaele for me; for Simpson the war finished there.

It was soon up the line again – on ground captured from the Germans. We had a primitive trench system in front of the villages of Wancourt and Guemappe with the Germans on a ridge some 800 yards away, while to the south the Australians were hammering away at the main Hindenburg line at Bullecourt and not very successfully. What we did not know was that there had been a large scale mutiny in the French army and this was the reason why the only partly successful Arras attack had to be continued. Our Division was to have another go on May 3rd, our battalion objective being the trench system covering the Arras-Cambrai road including the strong post St. Rohart farm.

We went up in daylight to reserve trenches passing massive artillery concentrations with guns wheel to wheel along the Tillois road and passing large numbers of the still unburied horses of the Life Guards decimated by shrapnel three weeks before. There was heavy shelling of our reserve trenches which were quite a mile or more from our new front line and the next day there was quite a surprise; there was the padre in full regalia coming across the open ground to hold a communion service in the reserve trenches. I am afraid that to me, even with my new religious enthusiasm, it looked rather theatrical and it seemed wrong, as not only was it emphasising the division between the sheep and the goats but the next day we were going to kill our Christian German brothers. After only a few weeks of being back to orthodox religion it was disconcerting, but for the moment I did not dwell on it.

That night we went out into No Man's Land to dig jumping off trenches as we were too far away from the new German position. Picks and shovels were issued and out we went to the sloping ground which rose to the Arras-Cambrai road position near the ridge. Fritz was throwing over a lot of heavy stuff into Wancourt and Guemappe just behind us. We started digging with the shells groaning and whistling overhead and exploding about 600 yards to our rear and it was most uncomfortable. Fritz must have had a patrol out and heard the noise we were making and in about twenty minutes the range shortened and we were really under shell fire.

It was a nasty night with a direct hit about 200 yards to the left and an immediate shout for stretcher bearers. The trouble was that we could not get much cover, as after about two feet of top soil we were in solid chalk and even with a pick could make very little impression. Captain Williams was pacing up and down and I remember as one salvo shrieked near he snatched my pick and started furiously hacking away. I always found it most nerveracking not to flatten out under shell fire and I knew he could not stay standing doing nothing and just waiting for the next salvo. They were not whizzbangs but 5.9s. The 5.9 was a very unpopular shell, came from the Germans' best gun and made a very large hole.

There were a few more casualties and we made very little impression on the chalk so after about another hour we packed up. I remember saying to our sergeant that with only about two feet of cover this trench would give us a hell of a good start. It is always the lining up on tapes or in jump-off trenches before the dawn attack which is so nerveracking. At zero hour all machine-guns are silenced by the deluge of shells of the modern barrage but before an attack there are continuous bursts of fire for an hour or two before dawn and this attack had certainly been well advertised. We went back to the reserve trenches and at dawn a most unusual thing happened; a terrific barrage opened up and we saw numerous green S.O.S. flares going up from the German positions. It was the first time we had ever had a trial barrage the morning before the appointed day and we thought it was stupid because it was also a rehearsal for Fritz and he pounded us for about an hour. Actually that was the idea as our planes were up spotting the latest German artillery positions.

The attack on the following morning May 3rd was on a front of about fourteen miles and although German positions were captured with a number of small successes this battle must generally be deemed a failure as there was no breakthrough. Zero hour was at the unprecedented time of 3.45 a.m. It was a surprise attack in the dark. The idea was not a good one, as there had been no preliminary training for an attack of this kind. Moreover it had been overlooked that at 4 a.m. there would be a moon setting immediately behind the attackers which would silhouette them.

Under the cover of a terrific barrage which gave the Germans no option but to keep down, there was little trouble in taking over the German advanced trench system with a few casualties and an advance of about 800 yards was made to a point near Rohart factory on the border of the Arras-Cambrai road. Then the advance was held up by heavy machine gun fire from the flanks, so other advancing troops must have been held up. It was then a matter of consolidating and holding on; the position occupied must have been in some sort of dead ground as throughout the day there was little action by the German artillery.

In all these advances in siege-like warfare there is always a lull when the artillery of both sides have no accurate knowledge of the ground not taken in an attack. Ground flares were always carried to be lit at the farthest point of advance, for spotter planes to inform the artillery of the new range of fire, but with attack and counter attack, ground flares can cause an awful lot of confusion. The Germans always seemed much more expert in the use of flare signals. As usual it is the machine gun which takes over, and on this day it was the flank machine gun fire which stopped any further advance.

There was a heavy counter attack about 10 p.m. which was at first partly successful but the position was to some extent restored. It was all very confusing and some time later the order was given to withdraw because the tongue of land captured could not have been defended against a strong attack. Considering it was a major attack the casualties were not very heavy, but just outside battalion H.Q. on the Wancourt road a shell landed on 'A' Company amd killed a very popular officer. We went back to the army barracks in the large square in Arras. Even there it was a bit jumpy as Fritz was putting over some long range high velocity shells, two of which hit the barracks. This was a new gun – you heard the gun fire, even miles away and the shell arrived almost as soon. It was boom-zip-bang almost as quick as you could say it and the suddenness made it a most unpopular weapon.

Soon we went further back to another camp and with the Arras battle still going on there was plenty of air activity. At this camp we had a good view of some seven silver observation balloons ('sausages') and on one fine evening we saw a low flying British plane come over the camp which went towards the left one of the string of balloons. We could see incendiary bullets leaving the plane

The ruins of the village of Poelcappelle. Two German concrete blockhouses destroyed by British gun fire. The large blockhouse in the distance was still occupied by the Germans. The photograph was taken on 13th September 1917 under German observation.

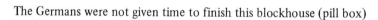

The Germans were not given time to finish this blockhouse (pill box)

Passchendaele fields, grassless, shell-holed and soggy earthed.

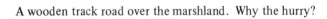

A wooden track road over the marshland. Why the hurry?

and almost immediately the balloon went up in flames with the two observers coming away in parachutes. Then the pilot shot up the next, and the next, and the next right to the end of the string. They were at least half a mile or so apart, but by the time he reached the third balloon all the observers were in the air parachuting down; it was a lovely sight and the sky was resplendent with seven great blobs of smoke. The pilot was of course a German in a captured British plane and he got clean away over the German lines. Years later, I read of this incident in someone's published war memoirs.

Our camp was in almost unspoilt country. It was not difficult to wander off on one's own, to sit in a field, to think, and read a little from *Golden Treasury*. It was a beautiful spring and one felt for the fields, flowers and trees just as Richard Jeffries felt. I found this out later as I only discovered Jeffries' *Meadow Thoughts* and *The Story of my Heart* after the war. Seeger's poem 'I have a rendezvous with Death' found a constant echo in my mind. Time could be running out and there was an intense and heightened awareness of life – all life. For me, it was the dawning of reverence for life so ably explained by Schweitzer's essay which I read many years later. Reverence for life in a bloody war – what irony. Pessimism? I suppose so, but there appeared to be no escape; it was death or a blighty wound and the margin between one or the other seemed to get narrower and narrower.

In that beautiful spring of 1917 how much we all wanted to live and how we cursed the war which by now we felt had nothing to do with us. I understand that for every single infantryman in the line there were eight men behind him. The eight may not have felt so disillusioned and bitter, but the P.B.I. did feel that way. The impersonal official histories never mentioned this aspect, but I must make it quite clear that when out on rest we were elated to the nth degree. Never before, or indeed in the years after the war did one have such a surge of joy in the appreciation of life. For the time being we were really cheerful; joked, laughed and enjoyed every minute and I must reiterate again that this is where the war correspondents' legend of patient and cheerful troops originated. It was of course the mental release, which with violent death always looming so near soon vanished on the return to the front line. The truth is that it was joy and despondency – up and down – up and down.

I have just been reading another book written a long time after the end of the war, by a survivor with rosy-tinted spectacles which emphasises the 'out on rest' attitude and plays down the 'up the line' ordeal. I feel this is a disservice to those who suffered so I must continue to write what was for me and my friends the true outlook of the soldier in the line.

Our changed mental attitude on rest showed itself in the ironical two edged comic songs which were sung with such gusto such as:

> I want to go home, I want to go home,
> I don't want to see the trenches no more
> Where there are whizbangs and shrapnel galore
> Take me over the sea where the Allemande can't get at me
> Oh my I don't want to die
> I want to go home.

And the ribald unprintable ditties such as the tribute to the sergeant major:

> You've got a kind face you old bastard,
> You ought to be bloody well shot,
> You ought to be tied to the door of a shit house
> And left there to bloody well rot ... etc.,

Parodied hymns were great favourites; for example 'What a friend we have in Jesus' was the tune for:

> When this bloody war is over
> Oh how happy we shall be,
> When I get my civvy clothes on
> No more soldiering for me ... etc.

Arras, 1917

To the tune of 'The Church's one foundation' we sang:

> We are Fred Karno's army the famous infantry,
> We cannot shoot, we cannot fight, what bloody use are we,
> And when we get to Berlin the Kaiser he will say
> Hoch Hoch mein Gott what a bloody fine lot are the boys of the
> L.R.B.

'Sing me to sleep' was the tune for:

> Far far from Ypres I want to be
> Where German snipers can't get at me
> Dark is my dugout, in there I creep
> Waiting for someone to put me to sleep.

Then there were the marching songs like 'Tipperary', 'Goodbyee', the sentimental songs, 'When you come home', 'Keep the home fires burning', 'Take me back to dear old blighty', 'If you were the only girl in the world', and so on.

Talking of songs and singing, we were lucky to have in our Lewis gun team a real character, Holmes; he was a composer and song writer – a very sensitive and music loving type and great company. When the battalion was out of the line on marches there was always the perpetual nag about keeping the step. The bugle band was the enemy as when we had got into a nice two mile an hour slouch, the bugle band would strike up and shouts of 'Left right – left right – pick it up' – went right down the slouching lines. The band nearly always got the bird from us which made our Colonel hopping mad; he used to gallop down the marching lines on his lovely black polo pony red in the face with exasperation. We had dire warnings in battalion orders but it never wholly stopped. Holmes thought he would write a satirical marching song for the Lewis gun team. The satire was more in the tune than in the words for he chose the banal 'Careless idle maidens' tune from *Faust* which was really ridiculous for fighting soldiers. The words we sang were:

99

Careless idle maidens wherefore sleeping still
The L.R.B. in glory is marching oe'r the hill,
The little birds are singing and hear what they do say
The Lewis gunners of five platoon are holding the step to-day.
Ta-ra-ra boom de ay ... etc.,

It was a great success.

We were a team of good companions while we survived. Even after all these years I cannot recall the chicken dinner episode without laughing. Holmes, Simpson, myself and someone else decided to have a celebration dinner. Holmes found a farm nearby run by an old woman and he paid for a chicken and arranged a meal which was to be served in the orchard that night – we would bring the booze. It was a lovely evening and with the rough table and chairs under an apple tree, a beautiful setting. The formidable old girl came out – first with the vegetables, and then with the *pièce de résistance* – the bird, and by God it proved to be a *pièce de résistance*. Holmes in his usual inimitable style of under statement said he had never met anything like it. Its head and neck were still attached and probably its innards were still inside. That was only the beginning. He went into the attack with a large carving knife but he simply could not cut it up.

At last, muttering, 'This one started life during the Crimean war,' he got the knife in the bird, raised it aloft and marched round us, singing to the tune of the Soldier's chorus from *Faust*, 'All bones and bloody great lumps of fat'.

It was one of the funniest things I have ever been mixed up with and I finished writhing on the ground – nearly a hospital case.

The old woman eventually came out, very perturbed, saying 'No bon? No bon?'

Holmes' reply was, 'You've said it! No bloody bon.'

He went back to the farmhouse, I presume had words and came back with some fat pork, and we had a damned good time on a never-to-be-forgotten evening in a French orchard. Simpson and I survived the war, Holmes and his friend did not.

100

Well, this lovely spring rest period was drawing to a close, and we heard the disappointing rumour that we were going back to the Arras front for another over the top. This is the time for the return of that peculiar sinking feeling; one does not show it, but it is there. Light heartedness goes, and there is more irritation and the nagging thought of – how long will this up to the front and out again last, it cannot go on for ever. We marched up to the deep reserve billets in ruined Achicourt, a suburb of Arras and then we were told that the over the top stunt was off. The piece of front line we took over was below the Vis-en-Artois ridge and approached by a long hastily dug shallow communication trench which the Germans had properly covered with a battery of whizzbangs which were the equivalent of our 18 pounder light field gun. We went up at dusk and it was a very nasty journey; one salvo made a direct hit and killed a number of chaps in A Company. Our narrow, deep hastily dug front line trench had not one scrap of barbed wire in front, and one feels quite exposed without the barbed wire barrier.

During the next few days we were really pasted by Fritz and we had never had such a volume of shells on a static trench system before. The still air was hazy with the fumes of explosions. One night it seemed certain that he was going to attack and owing to the intensity of the shell fire some officer prematurely put up S.O.S. rockets, (two greens and one red on this occasion). This is always disastrous for the P.B.I. on both sides, because both sides open up on the front line and so often it is a false alarm resulting in quite a number of unnecessary casualties.

I always remember that night, because for the first and last time I felt that it didn't matter a damn whether I was killed or not – my religious faith was at its maximum and I stood on our improvised fire step under the intense shell fire looking out while the rest of the lads were in the bottom of the trench. I surprised myself and possibly the rest of the platoon and luckily was not hit; it never happened again. After that night I was my usual self, and for the rest of my time in France.

It was here that we had our first taste of air attack on infantry in the trenches. A German plane swooped low over our trench, dropping a couple of light bombs and loosing off his machine-gun. This happened on three days and was most unexpected and unpleasant. The time came when we were relieved and going down the communication trench the damned whizzbang salvos took a heavy toll of seven platoon. I remember, with some surprise, because of the risk involved, that volunteers were asked for to fetch down some bodies. We thought that burial on the spot by the troops unlucky enough to be there was the proper procedure; there were enough dead without asking the men who for the moment were relatively safe to go back to that inferno.

Well, that was the end of the 1917 battle of Arras for our Division. It had been a failure. During the first twenty four hours on April 9th/10th a sizeable gap was made in the German defence line by the Canadians, but the cavalry had been held too far back. After the initial success with the capture of Vimy Ridge it might appear that the battle could well have been broken off and not ended up as the usual battle of attrition that all these offensives became.

Unfortunately, the Arras battle had to be continued because of the failure of the French Nivelle offensive which was to have been a joint action with ours. In the first forty-eight hours this much advertised battle was to have cracked wide open the German defensive system. Instead of victory the French infantry were mown down in their thousands by concentrated machine-gun fire from undestroyed concrete forts or pill boxes as we called them. The French theory of attack, attack, attack, had caused them to suffer huge losses in August and September 1914. Then Verdun in 1916, and the terrible winter of 1917 with insufficient leave for the front line troops, had left morale at a very low ebb.

All this smouldering unrest was sparked off by the failure of the Nivelle offensive and the great mutiny commenced. Fruitless attacks with huge casualties were continued after the initial failure until at last the infantry just refused to become cannon fodder. Elements of over fifty divisions were involved, and it was amazing that so little leaked out. Over 20,000 men were found guilty of mutiny in some degree and over 400 were sentenced to death; most of these, however, were deported to French prisons abroad and less than 100 were shot. The Germans had no inkling, otherwise the war might have been over in 1917.

Even Haig, a hundred miles away was not fully aware of the magnitude of the mutiny and it has been said that Haig, having been sworn to secrecy by Pétain let the minimum of information leak through to Lloyd George. It was the best kept secret of the war. With Pétain in charge and ringleaders being ruthlessly executed or imprisoned (some local commanders in the field were said to have chosen men at random for summary execution) the mutiny was eventually mastered. The infantry got their seven days' leave every four months (I had ten days in fifteen months) but the French army as a fighting force was completely finished during the summer and autumn of 1917 so we had to keep at it.

This time we went a long way back to a village called Sombrin and again life was really good. We had a first class barn with plenty of straw, good food, with even roast beef instead of eternal stew because the cooks built a field oven. The one blot on the landscape came when one day we were detailed to work on the nearby French farm. This did not sound too bad, but in effect it was. We started at 8 a.m. weeding and hoeing mangolds in a very large field. It was back aching and in the hot sun one hour was enough for me, but we went on until noon and then hied to the farm kitchen where we had a thin watery soup in which the main course had been boiled – salt pork! It was then back to work and at 6 p.m. we had really had enough and packed up despite the farmer's protests.

We had not been back in the billets more than half an hour before the sergeant came tearing in to ask what the hell we thought we were doing. We told him. He said the farmer had paid for our help and we had to go back. It was 8 p.m. before we were released. For three days we stuck it. We were absolutely fuming at being asked to work a twelve hour day after what we had been through – no rest – and getting none of the money the farmer paid for us. So, on the fourth day we went to the farm and just wouldn't work. There was one hell of a row but they couldn't make us work – we just went through the motions and we won because the farmer wouldn't have us.

This small strike stirred up a hornet's nest, particularly as the Army Staff had agreed to the utilisation of troops for farm work. Our point was that it was a damned disgrace to make front line troops work a twelve hour day when out on their hard earned rest. Why not put some of the eight men behind each front line man on the job? This long discourse about a minor incident may seem out of place but it was typical of the gulf and lack of understanding between General Staff and front line troops. It was, however, a grand rest period despite the farm episode and we had a most interesting sports day at the nearby château in Grand Rullecourt.

Then we were off north to the dreaded salient by the usual Pullman express to a village well back from the front for further training and preparation. I remember the sudden outburst of refresher courses, of rifle drill and shooting. It was quite true that the rifle was so little used in trench warfare that the finer points of adjusting sights for the range and allowance for wind etc., had almost been forgotten. Mills bombs were the trench weapon and we were told of the occasion when troops under counter attack even forgot to use the rifle at long range but waited until the enemy were well within bombing range.

I had a great surprise one night when my father appeared outside the barn. He was in the Royal Engineers stationed at Audruieq some three miles away and I arranged to go over one day. This I did and we had photographs taken and I heard from him about the masses of casualties passing through this railhead from the opening battle of the Ypres offensive on July 31st.

There were a lot of gas casualties as the Germans were using a new type of gas shell, so we had rather a panic exercise to attach another section of chemicals to our already large box respirator. It was a fine respirator, much better and more efficient than the German gas mask.

Simpson was now corporal in charge and I was No 1 and had to carry and fire the Lewis gun. No 2 carried the spare parts and loaded the magazines on to the gun and there were four others in the team who carried panniers of ammunition. No 2 was Canning, a very happily married man, with a son Tim on whom he doted, and we had all seen the family photographs. He felt his position very keenly and was not very happy even when out on rest. Perhaps he had a foreboding like so many had.

The Division was soon on the move and we finally reached a camp in Abeele where we stayed for the few days before we went up to the attack. Knowing the slaughter going on a few miles away and how the tanks had been swallowed up in the mud and hearing the incessant roar of the guns we were all very moody and apprehensive. This was increased by the leak, too soon, that the second big attack was to be about the middle of August and that our Division was to form the southern flank of the attack.

It has always been a question whether the semi-circular salient round Ypres should ever have been held and how many casualties would have been saved in the ensuing years after 1914 if the line had been consolidated on the Ypres-Comines canal which runs through Ypres. Be that as it may, the Germans in holding all the ridges to the east of Ypres had full observation over all activities in the area. In this flat country the rise of a few feet in the contours made a ridge invaluable for observation. There was nothing which could be called a hill – just ridges.

The Third Battle of Ypres, 1917, was well advertised by the preliminary action of the capture of Messines Ridge on the southern flank of the salient on 7th June 1917. In this attack, limited to two or three days' fighting, nineteen huge mines were exploded under the German positions on about a ten mile front and the ridge was captured with an advance of about two miles at the deepest point of penetration. Unfortunately there was an interval of six weeks before the main Ypres offensive opened. The object of the exercise was to gain the higher ground and combine this attack with one on the coast and so capture the Belgian coastal strip which was so useful to the Germans in their submarine campaign. Unfortunately part of this plan was forestalled by a German attack at Nieuport on the 10th July.

The battle of Pilkem Ridge, the first battle of Third Ypres, opened on 31st July. The preliminary bombardments combined with the heavy rains had turned the ground into a morass which proved a graveyard for our tanks. The maximum gain was about $1\frac{3}{4}$ miles in the centre and north, but the higher ground at Gheluvelt with Glencorse and Polygon Woods could not be taken. In subsequent days of bitter fighting Westhoek ridge was captured, but no impression could be made on the strong defences in the woods.

That was how we came to be lined up on Westhoek ridge for the attack on those heavily defended woods and which after two days' postponement because of the terrible state of the ground was fixed for August 16th. Our Division was to attack on a front of about 1500 yards and form a defensive flank of about 1700 yards up to the racecourse in Polygon Wood which was about one mile from our starting point.

The flank attack, or the attack to form a flank, was always chilling news because the troops chosen to form a flank are the suicide troops, and fifty per cent casualties could be optimistic. Early counter attacks are the rule and the bending back of a flank to form an arc even after a successful attack is usual.

The ground slopes gradually up to the right to the crest of Polygon Wood and this was the hinge that the Germans must hold, so the concrete block houses – pill boxes we called them – were formidable. The large ones are like miniature forts holding say thirty men and with five machine-guns. Ten years later in 1927 I took a photograph of the one on the north corner of Glencorse Wood. The concrete was yards thick and the volume of fire from that one alone could decimate a brigade. Proper trenches were impossible in this swamp and the way the Germans had fortified this area with these low flat pill boxes which were difficult to see was devilishly ingenious; it required the direct hit of a heavy shell to crack them.

It was not until five weeks later September 20th that this few hundred yards of wood and swamp were captured and that was accomplished only by replanning the method of attack i.e. one with a very limited objective and two or three shells for every yard of ground so that machine-gunners in the pill boxes were concussed and knocked semi conscious.

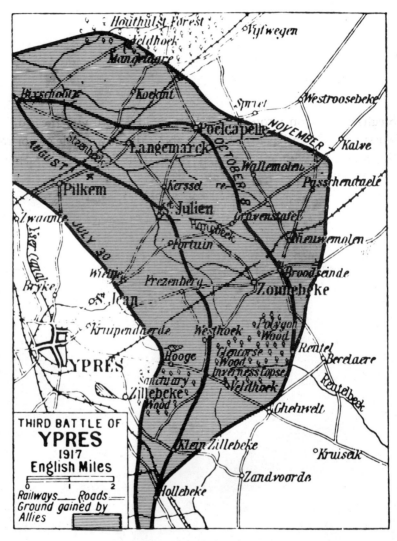

The Battle of Passchendaele
(Third Ypres)

CHAPTER 8

Passchendaele 1917

Siegfried Sassoon wrote of this battlefield, 'Here was the world's worst wound', and as I try to write about the unwritable or portray the unportrayable, I realise again the limitations of prose, the poets do it much better. It was about the biggest hell yet made by man for lingering death and shattered minds. Perhaps a day to day account would be the best way to describe my part in this offensive.

August 13th

It had been raining on and off for some days, but as we marched away from Abeele it eased off to give a dark damp afternoon with plenty of low cloud. On the corner of the road to take the salute, was our Colonel to see us march by. I had never seen him so moved and I swear there were tears in his eyes. I said to Simpson, 'I don't like that, I bet we are for it', and Simpson's reply was, 'How unlucky can you be, the bloody right flank'.

Some time after passing through Dickebush and with ruined Ypres on our left about a mile away, we came to a wooden plank road. Battle formation with considerable intervals – about a hundred yards between platoons was the order. That wooden plank road – what a sight it was – it was really shattering even after nine months of war horrors, it was unbelievable. On each side as far as the eye could see there was a swamp of shell holes mostly filled with water; there was not one inch of ground which had not been turned over. Each side of the road was littered with dead mules in all stages of decay, some green, some black, some with eighteen pounder shells still in the mule pack half buried in mud and the smell of decay on that warm damp August day stank to high heaven. There was no time or place for burying men or mules and how thankful we were for the low cloud as not one shell came over.

After what was an age of apprehension we reached slightly higher ground. This was rightly named Hell Fire Corner and the whole landscape was just a churned up heap of mud with not a vestige of green and on the left was what remained of the notorious Menin road.

In another few hundred yards we were at a sacking-curtained entrance to Half Way House. The curtains over the entrances were to keep out gas. This resting place was all underground and there was nothing to be seen on top except the entrance to steps which led down thirty or forty feet into the bowels of the earth. It smelled dank and musty and pumps were working night and day to keep the water away. The whole battalion and perhaps others were down there in this vast excavation safe from shell fire and we settled down for an uneasy night's sleep.

August 14th

The next morning, sergeants and runners went off to contact the troops ahead who we were to relieve and arrange for the scouts to lead us to Westhoek Ridge which was our battle position. They all came back safely later in the day having run the gauntlet of some very heavy shelling and they looked very grim. The afternoon was dry and brighter, so a number of us came out from the smelly underground cavern and sat on the top watching ambulances dodging shells on the Menin road to our left. Our Colonel and some officers also came up and were sitting not more than thirty yards away.

Then all of a sudden, with no warning, there was the wrong 'un – the scream of a shell right on top of us. It pitched not more than twenty yards away but luckily our group was under the blast and hawky pieces but it killed two and wounded others farther away. The Colonel was hit (I think it was his seventh wound) and rushing

110

for the steps right behind him I nearly knocked him down the steps. We soon heard that he was not badly wounded, but that he would be a hospital case and would not be with us for the attack. In the early evening just before it got dark, we splashed through the mud to a store near Zillebecke lake to pick up bombs and ammunition. As I looked round in the dusk, what an area of bleak desolation it was and with the lowering clouds which had an ominous yellow tinge over Ypres the whole thing seemed unreal. It looked like a picture of hell; this was not our earth, it was another planet. At about 9 p.m. we were ready to go up to Westhoek Ridge which was I suppose some 3½ miles ahead. We were in battle dress of course – no overcoat but with a haversack containing iron rations i.e. a tin of bully beef and hard biscuits exactly like dog biscuits, and not forgetting my mascot *The Golden Treasury*.

It was a pitch black night, and slipping, sliding and cursing we picked our way through the mud. I had put the 29 pound weight Lewis gun on a sling so as to have both arms free but the unbalance was my undoing and I slipped into a flooded shell hole, gun and all. The lads picked me out and the first job now would be to clean the gun as it was too muddied up to fire. My boots and puttees were, of course, sticky with wet mud – uncomfortable but they would soon dry out.

We must have halted for ages in the notorious Sanctuary Wood area, which was now no wood but shattered stumps of trees from three to eight feet high, and the ground was littered with broken timber and bodies. Twice I tried to sit on a tree trunk but only sat on a dead man. The difficulty was not only of maintaining contact but of standing upright in the slime. Somehow the scouts had lost the track which should have been taped, and probably was but the tape had been obliterated by the mud and we seemed to be wandering about in that morass all night.

It took about four hours to cover the 3½ miles from Half Way House to Westhoek Ridge. This so called ridge was only a few feet above the surrounding country but in this flat country even a few feet constituted a ridge. We were muddied up, wet, exhausted and

111

frustrated with this preliminary ordeal.

August 15

1 a.m. Some machine gun bullets were whistling around from a
few bursts from the Germans but nothing serious and in any case
we were too damned tired to care. In all this battle area the
approach to the front line positions is over open ground as there are
no communication trenches. It was still pitch black when suddenly
we tumbled into some connected shell holes which were the front
line on Westhoek ridge to the accompaniment of curses from the
troops we were relieving for making, as they said, 'too much bloody
noise'. We flopped exhausted into the deepest though narrowest
part of this shell hole trench system.

As dawn came we looked around, it was just a graveyard with a
pair of boots sticking out of the muddy mound on which I had been
lying and a couple of yards away there was another partly buried
booted foot and a shattered Lewis gun. A peep over the top, and
there about three hundred yards away was the devastated
Glencorse Wood; the wood that would seal the fate of so many of us
on the morrow. It must originally have been rather a dense wood
but the trees had all been beheaded and what was left was
shattered trunks like scaffold poles from three or four feet to ten feet
or more high.

A short peep from time to time was all that one could take, as
from somewhere among those treetrunks the Germans were
occasionally sniping, but the worst thing was the bodies lying
everywhere; they must have been mown down. For days this slight
ridge had been the scene of hellish attack and counter-attack and
the dead littered around were nearly all our chaps. Further out in
No Man's Land some might have been still alive as we had heard a
few odd noises like groans in the night, and the horrible smell of
decay in that warm damp August weather was everywhere.

As the morning wore on, the desultory shelling became more
intense but most of the shells were pitching about thirty or forty
yards behind us and then the range shortened and some near

misses made us very jumpy. Everyone in the team was chain smoking, a sure sign of tension. Your fingers dig into the soil as you hear the scream of a near miss and the tension grows as the damned shells explode and hawky bits descend on you.

Despite this shelling, the first job to be done was to clean the Lewis gun and make it workable again. That done, we sat close, touching one another as the trench shell hole was deeper in one corner. Canning, right in the corner, was the only man who could comfortably stretch out his legs; next to him was Saunders, then me, then Corporal Simpson, then Howard, and the quiet one; I forget his name, but if ever a man knew his number was up he was that man. He had seemed numbed and had hardly talked ever since we left Abeele.

Canning was reading a letter from home and had just been asked to move to give someone else a leg stretch in the corner. I remember he said, 'Just another minute' when there was the split second shriek of the direct hit; always it was a fraction of a second. I remember a blinding flash, being buried up to my arm pits and feeling a blow on my elbow.

My first thought was – I'm still alive and thank God I've probably got a Blighty one. Unfortunately it was not, it was just a speck of shrapnel which hardly drew blood. Our platoon officer Armstrong with the bombing section came round the corner to dig us out and I was soon free. On my right was Saunders with a piece of shell in the side of his face and yelling so loudly that I should have thought the Germans would have heard him. Canning, one yard away from me, was underneath a pile of earth, on my left Corporal Simpson was stretched out unconscious, Howard was O.K..and the quiet one quite dead with a head wound; so the Lewis gun team was now two strong.

I shall always remember the lads digging away with the Germans taking occasional pot shots. Armstrong dug up what at first looked like a flattened German helmet, in fact someone said that it was a German helmet, but it was Canning's – a flattened shape and he had been neatly beheaded. I thought Armstrong was going to pass out. They had to continue digging to extract Saunders' legs from underneath Canning and it was a mess getting his legs from Canning's trunk which was a horrible sight. One leg was twisted round the knee but luckily he passed out and stopped yelling. Our stretcher bearers had not yet been used so they were available for Saunders and Simpson. Simpson remained unconscious but we could not find a wound and they were lucky, because I believe that they were both taken back at dusk – so many totally incapacitated never got back.

We pushed the quiet one over the back of the trench and all we could do with Canning was to put just a thin covering of earth over him and sit on top as to have put more earth on would have made the hole too shallow for safety – that is, relative safety, as it would have been impossible to conjure up a more unsafe area than Westhoek Ridge on that day. There is no doubt that a shattered concrete emplacement nearby, helped to give the Germans an accurate range for that part of the ridge. We found the gun undamaged, requiring another clean up but only three intact magazines instead of at least twenty and in any case there was no one left to carry them so we had less than 150 rounds which could be fired in about sixteen seconds.

The rest of the day went in a dazed sort of way with shells pitching round either just in front or just behind. The near miss scream of those damned shells and the tension was the worst I had ever known; another direct hit seemed inevitable – the tale that no shell pitched in the same place twice was no consolation. The trouble was not to lose control – clench fists until the fingernails bite into the flesh – tighten the leg muscles – jaw muscles – any old thing to keep control. It was so terribly wearing. A bit of biscuit washed down with water was all the food eaten that day as no one could feel hungry under that shell fire. Philip Gibbs in his book *Realities of War*, in writing about the Irish Division next to us, says:

Every day groups of men were blown to bits until the ditches were bloody and the living lay by the corpses of their comrades.

Every day scores of wounded crawled back through the bogs if they had strength to crawl.

There was some commotion and yells on my right so I suppose that was another direct hit and I wondered whether anyone in the front line on the ridge would be left to go over at 4.45 a.m. the next day. I suppose all days must end and at dusk here it was, that split second scream of your very own shell, but it pitched about six yards away round the corner on the bombing section of our platoon. A moment's silence and round came Corporal West, very shaken but intact, saying, 'I believe they've all had it.'

Howard and myself went round to help and there were four of his bombing section in a muddled heap all dead; two bodies were really shattered, the other two at first sight looked untouched but were quite dead. Three of these four were up the line for the first time. The three others of the bombing section were wounded but not too badly and the lucky blighters were soon off back to safety. What we would have given to have been in their shoes.

Armstrong was there really shocked because he had taken a real mental and physical battering. A good officer becomes closely attached to his platoon and he kept repeating that half his platoon was three men. That is what he said to Captain Harper later that night and that the platoon was finished. Harper just said that he knew that we had to go over. I think we were all partly shell-shocked after that day's battering.

Those far away Generals who call shell shock cowardice should have had just one day on Westhoek Ridge. Again I have to reiterate what a travesty of justice were so many of the war time court martials; expediency was the only factor, not justice or mercy.

August 16th

White tapes had been laid out just in front of the trench to mark the first wave of the advance and as early as 3.30 a.m. we got out of the trench and lay down on the soggy earth. After that day's shelling and almost miraculous escapes I think I was past caring –

perhaps all of us on that bloody ridge felt the same.

We then started to throw up some earth with our entrenching tools to afford a meagre cover from the German machine-guns but luckily their range was just too high and the bullets were passing over us. These desultory bursts of fire went on most of the time. Sergeant Hobson was next to me and we talked our way through the waiting time. He explained again about the right-angled swing we were supposed to make, pivoting on Black Watch Corner: We both agreed that once the Germans knew that we were the right flank of the attack they would adopt the usual tactic of launching an immediate counter attack.

He was very pessimistic about the whole business and reckoned our chance of survival at about one in ten. The only thing to pray for was a quick one. We all had a horror of being badly wounded and taking days to die. I used a sling for the 29 pound Lewis gun as it was asking for trouble to carry it perched on the shoulder. A sniper's first priority is a machine-gun. On a sling it can still be effectively fired from the waist as a Lewis gun only vibrates when fired and there is no recoil. My revolver was the large Colt which I always carried cocked and dangling on the lanyard when going over the top and this precaution may have saved my life about an hour later.

Unfortunately we had no automatic pistols like the German Browning and it was difficult to hit anything with our Colts and Webleys unless they were cocked. Uncocked, they have a six pound pull and if excited one could miss a haystack. It is a strange experience lying there waiting for zero and one is very mentally alert – over-tensed, I suppose, beyond being frightened, just being resigned to the inevitable. Zero was at 4.45 a.m. and it seemed to get too light, particularly as there was a rising volume of machine-gun fire.

Suddenly, looking back, the whole horizon seemed to burst into flame as thousands of guns started the barrage. What a sight it is – there is the burst of flame right across the horizon behind, in seconds the whine of thousands of shells and then almost immediately the deafening crash of explosions. In front, the very earth disintegrates with everything going up and it is quite impossible to hear the loudest shout of the man next to you. I remember jumping up and shouting, 'Come on the L.R.B.' – a keyed up adrenalin reaction, as no one could hear me.

Then we were off at a slow walk, picking our way over the churned up earth. The ground made it impossible to continue in line and soon we were filing our way over obstacles and flooded shell holes. I remember jumping over a narrow trench filled to the brim with dead Germans and thinking just at that moment that they were tidier than us as they collected theirs. After hammering the front positions for a scheduled number of minutes according to the width of No Man's Land, a creeping barrage lifts at about twenty to thirty yards a minute, depending on the nature of the terrain and the first waves of attackers must be close enough to the barrage so that the Germans who must take cover from the devastating shell fire have no time to reorganise. Inevitably the front waves of advancing troops have quite a number of casualties from their own shells. Today the barrage seemed to lift quite slowly which was just as well because it was impossible to move quickly and hawky bits seemed to be sploshing into the marshy ground all around, but none hit me. The German counter-barrage started almost immediately with ours and we learned afterwards that this quick reply was due to the fact that the whole plan of our attack that day had been betrayed.

Into the shattered wood we went with no Germans visible and came upon a sunken farm road or track in the side of which there were entrances to a dugout. Sergeant Carter and his runner were first at the entrance and were immediately killed from shots from the dugout. There were some bombs thrown at the entrance and I got on the other bank of the sunken track and fired bursts from the Lewis straight down the dugout steps using most of the precious magazine.

They soon came up and the first one up in this situation is a very brave man as he has little chance of survival. What a crowd –

probably forty or fifty and of course they had had to take refuge as no man could have lived through that barrage in the open above ground. They had their hands up and appeared to have no weapons.

Then some of our men, I suppose it was their first time up and they were over-excited started shooting at them – good old propaganda – hadn't they been told that the only good German was a dead one? And lately it had been drilled into us on parade that we were short of food and that prisoners had to be fed. We, the old soldiers stopped them as soon as possible, and in any case the idiots could have hit some of our own advancing men.

Some men were detailed to take the prisoners back and this was always a ticklish job because of the counter-barrage. On we walked over tree trunks, shell holes and debris and for the moment there were no Germans visible. My No. 2, with two magazines had disappeared; he may have been shot or have lost touch, so my Lewis gun was going to be a museum piece. I had no loading handle and even with that the magazine has to be slowly loaded one bullet at a time.

No shells were falling near as our barrage had lifted and the Germans could not shell their own positions. It takes quite a time for the artillery to know the depth of an advance; however the noise, swish and shrieks of countless shells overhead were still there. Shells can never be seen in the air, they move too fast. This relative silence and release from immediate shelling in the vicinity is a feature of an attack of this kind, but then very quickly comes the ominous rat-tat-tat of the machine-guns, the real killer. It was a marvellous sunrise and I remember the huge red ball of the sun resting on the top of a distant pill box and an explosion and the clear silhouette of a man throwing up both his hands which I thought at the time was just like a painted picture of battle so dramatically portrayed in battle scenes of the Victorian era.

On we walked through the truncated wood, but the machine-gun fire rose to a crescendo and we seemed to be walking through a curtain of bullets. It was really devastating and chaps were dropping all over the place. There must however be no stopping even to look at anyone wounded. Captain Harper came rushing by with his arm smashed up and he shouted something to the effect about going back, it was hopeless, and that we were being surrounded. Somehow, however, we just went on walking and I also remember some time later the sergeant major appearing and shouting, 'Dig in – dig in!' – which was much easier said than done.

Then walking on, I do not know how far, I suddenly was alone, there was now no one near me. What had happened? Now the panic really started – this was it – and I changed direction to make for a shallow shell hole. As I did so, a bullet ripped through the case of the Lewis gun and it nearly swung me over but I made it. Later that change of direction was nearly my undoing as I had partly lost my sense of direction. The nearest men visible to me appeared to be another Lewis gun team, at least I thought I saw a Lewis gun and they were possibly some three hundred yards or so away and I saw them disappear into a hole. I could see no one else.

With my entrenching tool I tried to throw up more cover but all I dug into was the grey uniform of a dead German and maggots. The Lewis gun was useless, in any case I had no ammunition so I took off the feed arm, put it in my pocket, and smashed up the gun mechanism with my entrenching tool.

It was difficult to look round as bullets were flopping into the earth at the back of the shell hole and the machine gun fire pouring into the wood was the heaviest I had ever experienced, but in the lull when the sharp crack-crack sound had fallen to a lower tone I peeped out.

I appeared to be on one edge of the wood, the ground sloping down towards the Germans and open country, a flooded marshy area with dark blobs, which I supposed were pill boxes, just visible. There was no one apparently on the left so presumably the attack over that marsh had failed or had never really been able to start. I did not know what to do but to run the gauntlet of the machine-gun fire seemed suicidal.

Then there was a strange incident which I can never properly explain; I am sure that a man in a khaki coat rushed past me and towards the German pill boxes. Who was he? A German escaped prisoner was the most likely explanation or a man trapped by our barrage.

Time passed, how long I do not know, but I stayed cramped, crouched down in that shell hole with bullets plopping into the earth on the slight rising bank behind and I thought well this must be the end. Then away to my right in the direction of the Lewis gun team a green flare went up and then another and miraculously the machine-gun fire from the north east flank slackened and stopped. There were Germans coming through the south east corner of the wood in short rushes, as though they were on parade, it looked so disciplined. (Afterwards I learned they were *Stosstruppen Jaeger* storm troops.) They had reached the Lewis gun team and standing round the shell hole appeared to be shooting them; that must have happened for ten years later I looked for and saw the names of an 'A' Company Lewis gun team on the Menin Arch – men with no known graves.

Partly paralysed with fear I wondered what the hell to do and suddenly I was out like a flash and dashed towards a group of shattered tree trunks, but in the wrong direction as I was running right into a German behind a tree trunk. I just let off a shot with my cocked revolver and he appeared to drop and I bolted like mad in the opposite direction down a slight slope into the open country on the edge of the wood and towards the pill boxes. That stray German could have been one of the men caught in the wood when the attack started, or a stray from a dugout.

I then collected my thoughts, calmed down, and worked my way back along that lower edge of the wood and saw Corporal West, Armstrong and a sergeant also beating a hasty retreat. We covered the next few hundred yards in quick time and again got into the wood where remnants were still straggling back. With the Germans counter-attacking, all their flank machine-gun fire had ceased and we seemed relatively safe.

Further on, I remember a group with an officer firing at the distant advancing Germans over tree trunks, the officer was waving his revolver and saying in the old heroic tradition that he would shoot the next man who fell back. We took no notice – it was damned silly – there wasn't a hope in hell of holding an isolated position in that wood with an attack on our right and no support on our left. The attack on Glencorse and Polygon woods had been a complete failure. The counter-attack of the Germans had been mounted so quickly that it was unbelievable, but we did not know then that the Germans knew beforehand the full plan of the attack.

I carried on walking back, picked up a rifle and eventually reached almost the exact spot on Westhoek Ridge where I started. I jumped into the trench on top of the dead bombers, then went round the corner and sat down on top of Canning where I could stretch my legs and went to sleep! I do not know how long we had been in the wood – was it one hour, two hours or more – I did not even look at my watch but the tension had been such, I just had to sleep. There was no one near me, in fact all that day I was on my own with some men perhaps twenty yards or more to the left and right but out of sight. We had been terribly thinned out and I had no desire to talk to anyone or be with anyone.

I was awakened by a shower of muddy water; a light shell must have pitched into a muddy shell hole at the back. Half awake and still dazed I looked round and saw a piece of letter paper partly covered with earth. It must have been part of the letter Canning had been reading and I remember looking at it and seeing the words of the ending, 'May God bless you and keep you for Tim and me', and here he was under a few inches of earth with me sitting on top of him.

I shall never forget that bit of paper – it was the last straw. Looking back I am sure it was the turning point for me and many of my beliefs and I thought bitterly and cynically about what writers and poets had written glorifying war. Then the gist of Moore's '*Pro Patri Mori*' came to mind. I thought what nonsense it was in this setting – me sitting on top of Canning – boots sticking out of the earth and death all round. Where in God's name was the pride in dying for one's country?

Everything had now quietened down; no shelling of the ridge, even the guns were exhausted; there was only the droning of shells from the heavies overhead which were pitching two or three miles back. It was a strange, almost other-worldly, experience sitting in that shell hole trench for the rest of the day by myself and thinking about the chances of survival. I looked again at the boots sticking out of the mud – a flash to the Third Hour – 'My God, my God why hast thou forsaken us'. Where, oh where, was God in this earth covered ossuary – this mud swamp receptacle for the bones of the dead? It was I suppose for me the moment of truth. I thought of the patriotic national churches all praying for victory. How could God choose? We Christian killers killing Christians. Could there be a personal God who would listen to me if I regularly confessed to be 'a miserable sinner with no health in me'. I felt miserable enough but more sinned against than sinning.

I had had doubts before but I now saw clearly, I think for the first time, that the Church's teaching of personal salvation with all the emphasis on sin, forgiveness, confession, absolution was a selfish creed. If I survived I should have to find a more self-less religion than that of the Church – if I survived. As I have said before I have always been interested in, and a keen student of religion and now on this day, with this traumatic experience, my belief in a Church which condoned killing faded away. I would not again voluntarily attend or take part in the communion or other Church services, and rightly or wrongly that was that. Deep thinking on this day in this place of useless sacrifice, but would there ever be a more appropriate time and place?

Yet how do I reconcile this attitude with my action only a few hours later when with a newly acquired Lewis gun taken from a Queen Victoria rifleman, who would die a lingering death, I was trying to kill Germans who were jumping over an obstacle in the wood and possible preparing for an attack on the ridge. It was a dilemma which faced front line troops on both sides. They were sick to death of killing, but trapped in the war machine the only path left for survival was to get on with the killing and hope to survive. Why did I go on with the killing – I loved life too much to lay it down – I was not martyr material – and in any case it would have been a useless sacrifice. A common soldier could not take the stand which Siegfried Sassoon took when he lost faith in the aims of the war. If a common soldier on active service refused to fight for conscientious reasons he would unquestionably have been shot.

I do not remember eating that day but I got some water from a water bottle belonging to one of the dead bombers round the corner. It was a lovely warm summer day and later on in the afternoon I thought I heard a noise or groan coming from a narrow sap about a dozen yards away which ran out towards the wood, so I crawled up the sap to a shell hole and in it was a man of the Queen Victoria Rifles with a badly shattered shoulder. It was a shell wound and a real mess with blood all congealed. At first I thought he was dead, his face bloodless and white and his teeth were clenched; he was too far gone to talk but he just blinked his eyes at me. I shall always see him – those clenched teeth, white face, and the eyes, but I just took the Lewis gun which was by his side and was quite intact with a full magazine, and crawled back. I hope he soon died.

Why did I do nothing? There was nothing I could do. At least six men and a stretcher would be necessary and the journey to the battalion first aid post and then the slow struggle back to the advance dressing station would take hours. In this type of battle the opening barrages caused so many casualties that available stretchers and stretcher bearers are used up almost immediately. As I have previously mentioned, stretcher bearers are men from your own battalion who give up their arms and wear white arm bands with a red cross. The Royal Army Medical Corps trained staff are back at the advance dressing station where they take charge. In major attacks it is impossible to provide a sufficient number of stretcher bearers as there would be no one left to go 'over the top'.

In these battles the incapacitated wounded left in No Man's Land just died. Sometimes wounded men would be rescued if there was an early new attack. In the Arras battle my friend Morton was recovered alive after seven days' exposure, but it was weeks before another attack was launched from Westhoek Ridge.

This then was the desperate situation for the incapacitated wounded. There was no armistice to allow a search as in past wars when even at night searchers with lanterns scoured the battlefields. In this swamp of mud filled shell-holes the situation was more than desperate – it was appalling.

As I have already mentioned in the opening to this chapter, Siegfried Sassoon in his bitter poem about the Ypres battlefield wrote, 'Here was the world's worst wound', and for the wounded man faced with a lonely painful death, unable to struggle back through the slime and often taking days to die, it was all that. For those of us who saw it, lived amongst it, and survived, it would always be remembered as the supreme horror and degradation of Passchendaele – it was unforgettable – unforgivable.

Early on that summer evening a number of low flying German planes came right over us. At first I thought there might be an attack on the ridge as green marker flares were going up in the wood, (how expert the Germans were in their flare signalling) and I saw Germans getting over some obstacle between the shattered tree trunks probably on their way to their old positions in the sunken road. I hoped that was all, because we were in a very poor state to withstand an attack on the ridge. I fired a few bursts with my newly acquired gun which slowed them up considerably.

Soon it became dark and about an hour later someone came into my shell hole with a message that all L.R.B.s were to move up to the right. I moved up, joined a small group, and was told that we were being relieved. I could hardly believe it – it was wonderful news, a chance to live and I told a relief man about the wounded man in the sap. He said, 'What can I do – there are wounded all over the place out there.'

I soon joined a group of about ten or a dozen including Armstrong and a sergeant and when I asked about the rest he said that some had already gone on and that we had had a very bad day.

I knew that all right; so we trudged back over the newly churned up earth to try to find Half Way House. The ground was littered with new shell holes but it was drier under foot and although we got lost a few times through missing the markers after an hour or so of floundering we found the curtained entrance of Half Way House and tumbled down the thirty or forty steps to safety. It was so dark that one group, although only a few hundred yards away never found an entrance and all night they had to wear gas masks because of a gas shell bombardment.

August 17th

It was a snooze of complete mental and physical exhaustion and on waking there was only water and biscuits. One incident I clearly remember was our sergeant major saying, 'Form up on top and get ready to march back.'

I said to him, 'Good God, form up – can't we just get back?' and he said, 'All right, off you go.'

Unfortunately it was a fine morning and we were afraid of being caught on that wooden road but luckily no shells came over. The road had been badly smashed up in places; there were more dead horses in the marsh on the sides and some dead men who had been caught in the counter barrage fire of yesterday had been piled up for collection. The road to Hell Fire Corner – how well named – was in fact the road to about the biggest hell man had yet created.

We hurried desperately to get away for to have been pipped on that road after what we had been through would have been the supreme irony. The wooden track eventually joined up with a proper road and soon we were struggling past a battery of heavy guns. These chaps, coming to look at us, jaded, haggard and white faced remnants had the damned cheek to shout out something to the effect that we hadn't made it, and why hadn't we. That is when some of us really felt like murder and we would have liked to take that lot and stick them under the murderous machine-gun fire from pill boxes their guns had not smashed. Sir Philip Gibbs, the well known war correspondent, wrote this in his book *From Bapaume to*

Passchendaele 1917 when referring to the attack of 16th August:

It was on the right that the enemy fought hardest, counter attacked most fiercely and most often concentrated the heaviest artillery. There were the Irish brigades there, the 8th Division and the London battalions of the 56th Division. All this side became at once involved in desperate fighting. The ground was damnable, cratered, full of water, knee deep in foul mud, and beyond them was high ground stuck through with gully like funnels, through which the enemy would pour up his storm troops for counter attack; and away in the mud were the same style of concrete forts as up north and still unbroken by our bombardments with new garrisons of machine gunners. I know more about the Londoners because I have been to see them to-day … Lying out all night in the wet mud under heavy fire, they attacked at dawn up by Glencorse wood, in the direction of Polygon wood. On the right they and their neighbours at once came under blasts of fire from five machine guns in a strong point, and under a hostile barrage fire that was frightful in its intensity. They could not make much headway. No mortal man could have advanced under such fire and so their comrades on the left were terribly exposed to the scythe of bullets which swept them also.

I photographed this strong point on the corner of Glencorse wood ten years later in 1927. The concrete was yards thick and only dynamite would ever clear it.

For some time we straggled on further down the road and after quite a long way we came upon grass and trees and it was quite emotional to see the green grass and trees after the churned up mud of the salient. Eventually, in one of the fields there were our field kitchens and hot food and it was so good. After a rest we moved on to a camp of tents and barns and had a wash and brush up.

Later in the day we were paraded to hear a pep talk from Major Walker, the second in command, as our Colonel had been wounded. We had the usual blah-blah about doing it again if called upon and the surprising information that our lack of success was primarily due to the fact that a sergeant of the Welsh Fusiliers employed as a clerk at G.H.Q. had been returned to the line for disciplinary purposes and had deserted to the Germans, taking with him the plan of the attack.

At first we thought it was just a yarn to excuse our costly defeat but then we remembered the shells that dropped amongst us, and slaughtered the reserves behind us, at the very moment our barrage opened. This counter-barrage was too quick and the counter-attack from the right flank of Glencorse wood was also remarkably quick. Also I remembered that there was no one moving on our left when we were on the edge of the wood and shells and machine guns must have stopped that attack. Fifty years later the *Daily Telegraph* printed a letter from G.E. Mackenzie, Minister of Kirkhope, late of 153rd Brigade R.H.A., an extract of which is as follows:

... but thàt day something inexplicable happened. Within one minute of zero hour and the opening of our barrage it was replied to by artillery on the entire enemy front facing us. Our infantry were simply mown down by shell fire. The reason for this unparalleled readiness on the part of the Germans was only revealed when forty eight hours later I reported back to the battery. There I was shown a report captured from a German dugout in the front line which had been translated and circulated by our G.H.Q.

The night before, (August 15th) a sergeant of the Welsh Fusiliers who had been employed as a clerk at G.H.Q. and had been returned to the line for disciplinary purposes had treacherously deserted to the enemy taking with him not only information of tomorrow's attack, but also a copy of a map on which was indicated the position of every battery on that section of the British front.

However, apart from that, I doubt very much whether the attack would have succeeded. The objective, an advance of over a mile, was much too far away to cope with the devastating pill box defence and the new tactic of immediate counter attack. Lessons were learned which were put into practice on September 20th when the woods were captured and when there was a much more intensive artillery preparation on a shorter front and with the first objective only half a mile away instead of over a mile.

Never before had any battle affected our nerves so badly. Practically all the day there was the noise of shells, swish, swish, rumble, rumble in the ears. This had never happened before so we must have been suffering from severe mental shock. Quite a number of us survivors mentioned this. Neuralgia was so common that there was a queue at the medical tent for sedatives. I was going along a field path to the medical tent for tablets with another man when there was a sudden burst of machine-gun fire from a nearby practice firing range. We immediately dropped flat on the ground and how foolish we felt at this reaction miles behind the front line.

It was another proof that most of us were suffering from a type of shell shock and the sleeping tablets helped to ensure a better night's rest. Shellshock was a term widely and sometimes lightly used but the desire to flatten out even with a sharp noise or an order showed that damage, sometimes permanent, had been done to the nervous system. In after years neuropathic disorders were due to this experience.

Perhaps no normal infantry man who had been through a 1917 Passchendaele attack would ever be quite the same again. This was the battlefield of all battlefields which exposed the ultimate degradation of fighting and man's inhumanity to man. That is why such a detailed account has been written. Some might say how can all this detail be remembered. It can, because one is so emotionally charged and if one has a photographic type of memory every detail is there for life. Ten years later in 1927 I could pick out every place without hesitation, simply by the contour of the ground. It seems superfluous to write any more about that ghastly battlefield and words are so ineffectual. For me the one word is obscene and it was obscene to the nth degree.

In the preliminary bombardment in July about four and one

Stretcher bearers, two British soldiers and four German prisoners — the minimum six required for one casualty.

German prisoners and escort. What an unhappy lot.

Infantry digging out a ditched tank in an overrun cemetery.

The truly formidable barbed wire defence system of the Hindenburg Line. Only tanks could flatten it.

quarter million shells were hurled into the few square miles of land which was barely above water level. Then the rains came and it was impossible for any one person to get a wounded man back over that swamp. A stretcher and six men were necessary and about eight hours of time, so that after an attack, the cries and moans of the wounded in the new No Man's Land continued for days. In October, from the village of Passchendaele itself, it took about twelve hours. That is why there are 56,000 names in gold on the Menin Arch of men missing with no known graves. No wonder Siegfried Sassoon wrote his bitt bitter poem about the Menin Arch, no 'Glorious Dead', but:

Who will remember, passing through this Gate,
The unheroic dead who fed the guns?
Who shall absolve the foulness of their fate, –
Those doomed, conscripted, unvictorious ones?
Crudely renewed the Salient holds its own.
Paid are its dim defenders by this pomp;
Paid, with a pile of peace-complacent stone,
The armies who endured that sullen swamp.

Here was the world's worst wound. And here with pride
'Their name liveth for ever', the Gateway claims.
Was ever an immolation so belied
As these intolerably nameless names?
Well might the Dead who struggled in the slime
Rise and deride this sepulchre of crime.

It was an emotional moment standing on the top of that Menin Arch ten years later in 1927, looking out over the few square miles to the low Passchendaele ridge and then pondering on the tally – 160,000 British dead, about 100,000 German dead, over 400,000 British wounded, and about 200,000 German wounded, in these few square miles which could be seen from the top of the Arch. No wonder it was difficult to find earth and not dead men, as I found when digging for cover in Glencorse Wood. Later on that day in

1927 when, having taken photographs of the wood and the yards thick concrete pill box fort, which must have been the one that Philip Gibbs mentioned as containing five machine guns, I looked over the area from Westhoek Ridge with the setting sun and only a solitary ploughman in view, and meadow flowers growing around the shattered pillbox, I nearly broke down at the contrast of the peaceful scene with that of ten years before. Chekhov's emotive sentence at the end of one of his stories came to mind as it seemed so appropriate in this setting –

> However passionate sinning and rebellious the heart hidden in the tomb, the flowers growing over it peep serenely at us with their innocent eyes; they tell us not of eternal peace alone, but of that great peace of indifferent nature; they tell us too of eternal reconciliation, of life without end.

Well, it was an emotional thought which seemed a fitting conclusion to that day in 1927 on the lonely deserted battlefield.

But to go back ten years to 17th August 1917. There was now the difficult reckoning of those known to be killed. One had to be quite certain. The padre had the job of going round for names and being one of his flock he soon saw me and I told him of all those who I knew and had actually seen dead. I also told him of the shooting at Germans, Canning's letter and the Lewis gunner I left to die. From my manner I am sure the padre sensed my changed attitude, but he tried no platitudes. There was plenty of food – there always was after a big attack. The post had arrived and there was the routine distribution of the food contents of the parcels of casualties. Somehow it always seemed to be rather callous to be eating cakes etc., baked by wives and mothers of casualties.

The next day we marched off to the camp we had left a few days previously and heard the unwelcome news that we would soon be made up to strength and would probably return to the Salient. A return to that hell hole was too awful to contemplate and one man said he would not go despite the fact that he would probably be caught and shot. He was never tested because fortunately we did not go back. As I have said before this is not an account of heroes but of ordinary men caught up in situations often completely beyond anything they could have imagined. The truth is that before an attack the normal man is grey with fear – in the moment of attack he has no time for fear – and after the attack the reaction can be shattering. It takes all sorts to make our world. There is Julian Grenfell who was killed early in the war, and whose poem 'Into Battle' contains in one verse the lines:

And he is dead who will not fight;
And who dies fighting has increase.

And in another verse the lines:

And only Joy of Battle takes
Him by the throat, and makes him blind.

Had he survived another twelve months I would like to believe that he would have been so sickened by the slaughter that he would have written another poem in a different vein. Thank God that people so happy in war and happy in killing their own kind, are in the minority. Schweitzer's 'Reverence for Life' philosophy would make little impact on them – on the other hand, we have Wilfred Owen and Siegfried Sassoon giving us the true picture of the pity of war – the pity war distils. It does indeed take all sorts to make our world.

Lest anyone should think the foregoing account of Passchendaele 1917 is an exaggeration this is what Ludendorff said about the battle:

Enormous masses of ammunition, such as the human mind had never imagined before the war were hurled upon the bodies of men who passed a miserable existence scattered about in mud filled shell holes. The horror of the shell hole area of Verdun was surpassed. It was no longer life at all. It was merely unspeakable suffering. And through this world of mud the attackers dragged themselves, slowly, but steadily, and in dense masses. Caught in

131

the advance zone by our hail of fire they often collapsed, and the lonely man in the shell hole breathed again. Then the mass came on again. Rifle and machine-gun jammed with mud. Man fought against man, and only too often the mass was successful.

What the German soldier experienced, achieved, and suffered in the Flanders battle will be his everlasting monument of bronze, erected by himself in the enemy's land.

The enemy's losses were also heavy. When we occupied the battlefield in the spring of 1918 we encountered the horrible spectacle of many unburied corpses. They lay there in thousands. Two thirds of them were enemies, one third German soldiers who had found a hero's grave.

If Ludendorff knew this surely so did Haig. Only a few years ago Montgomery said in a radio interview that Haig had a complete disregard for human life. Also Major Dudley Ward said in his book *The 56th Division*:

> There is no place on the whole of the Western Front which can be compared to this stretch of Flanders. If an infantry man or artillery man attempted to give an adequate account of conditions and the horrors which they occasioned he would not be believed.

To sum up, Passchendaele was a sheer waste of man power. We lived in waterlogged connected shell holes while the Germans had developed an almost unbeatable system of defence to combat the conditions. They had their main troops ready to counter attack immediately the attackers had reached the limit of their advance and endurance. These were kept in reserve away from the initial barrage. Only 24,000 prisoners and 74 guns were captured in the whole period from July 31st to the middle of November in an advance which at the deepest part was only four and a half miles on a front fifteen miles long and at the cost of over half a million casualties. With their zonal pill box defence the German casualties were probably only about half of ours.

It is no use trying to whitewash Haig and the General Staff. This is usually done by arm chair tacticians who make judgments as if they were playing a game with toy soldiers, not human beings. After the first few days' abortive attempts at a breakthrough, nothing of value could be achieved. It became another bloody battle of attrition where so many wounded died lingering deaths in the mud. Third Ypres was a military crime. Haig's diary and the official accounts are monuments of understatement. He appeared to have no idea of front line conditions, possibly because his Staff Officers never saw the front line. No wonder Lieutenant General Sir Lancelot Kiggell broke down when he saw the swamp, saying, 'Good God, did we really send men to fight in that.'

Soldiers who had been out for some time and had survived knew we were only fighting for some power complex. I must reiterate we did not really hate the Germans, the hate was at home, manufactured and fomented by atrocity stories, the corpse factory lies etc. We, the old soldiers were always ready to give a prisoner a cigarette and reassure him. Contrast this with the men straight out from England, brainwashed with hate and slogans such as 'The only good German is a dead one – kill all Boche.' The longer these men survived, so their hate lessened.

This story is about the morale and thoughts of the front line soldier, so to conclude the account of this Passchendaele battle, what were his thoughts when lying in the mud during that hour before zero? They were not in accord with the war correspondents' stories about brave cheerful troops, or with that line of Lieutenant Colonel Seton Hutchison previously quoted, 'Here upon the highest peak of human history, yet unafraid, Warrior stands.' In justice to 'the unheroic dead who fed the guns' the truth must be told about these last moments. The thoughts were not about dying gloriously as the war memorials say, or of patriotically dying for King and Country. They were, if this is to be the end, it must be a quick one, not a lingering death in that swamp. If any of them were given the free choice of the cup passing from them in their Gethsemane they would all have taken the road not forward towards the pill boxes, but back to safety. How many would have been left to attack if there had been a less drastic alternative than the much publicised execution for deserters is the question.

Well then you will ask, why did men apparently unhesitatingly go forward in an attack and capture strong points sometimes with reckless bravery? The answer is simple – I must repeat that there is no alternative to the firing squad but to go forward and you do your damndest to kill the men who are trying to kill you. If you do not, you just die. In all this fighting when trenches and strong points are captured, you are not a hero – you are obeying not man's instinct to kill but man's instinct to live by killing the man who would kill you. Those who believe in the inevitability of war will always emphasise that man has an inherent killer instinct, that it is human nature and little can be done about it. Another 'Old Lie', a perfidious old lie. Man is not born a killer, it is the society in which he grows up which makes him one and that society must continually reiterate the lie to justify the act of killing in war and the profitable manufacture of the weapons to do that killing. I never wanted to kill anyone, but I did. I have no inherent killer instinct, neither had any of my companions throughout the war. In all my life, I have never met a man with the inborn instinct to kill other men.

CHAPTER 9

Cambrai 1917

Replacement troops soon arrived and the general reorganisation of the battalion commenced. This was rather a depressing time for the survivors as a number of close friends had gone and it meant a fresh start with new companions. As one of the two survivors of the platoon's Lewis gun section I was made lance corporal in charge of a new Lewis gun team. It was not a big promotion, but the only one I wanted, as of all the N.C.O. jobs I am sure it was the best. There was no rifle to carry, only a revolver, and as it was the most important section of the platoon it usually had the best bivvy in the line and missed most wiring and fatigue parties. The drawbacks were patrol jobs or holding advance listening posts, but on the whole it was a much more organised existence, and in normal trench warfare the Lewis gun N.C.O. after posting sentries for the night had all the night for complete rest. I suppose I was fortunate; I had two older men back from hospital after minor wounds and four new youngsters straight from England.

After a few days' rest it was the Pullman train and back to the camp near Audruieq which we had left a few weeks before. This was rather depressing because of the missing faces when we were billetted in the same barn. One day I decided to go to Audruieq to see my father and he was surprised to see me, as not having heard from me he thought I must have become a casualty particularly as the heavy losses in the 16th August attack was well known at this rail head.

We were only a few days in this area and then came the good

news that we were not going back to the salient but south, to the area in front of Bapaume with the Somme battlefield well behind us. We eventually finished up at the ruined village of Lebuquière about six miles east of Bapaume. This was our reserve headquarters for some months, in fact until we pulled out of this area in December 1917 after the Cambrai tank battle.

All this area was completely devastated right up to the front line which was about two to three miles further on. This was not caused by fighting but by the German scorched earth policy. Villages were simply burnt or blown up and where possible all trees and bushes destroyed. About a mile away was the small village of Beaumetz-les-Cambrai and it was a strange sensation when slogging back from the front line to pass through this ghostly village in the moonlight with a roadside altar and crucifix still intact. The ghostly windowless devastated houses made one wonder whether one had passed over into another world.

The next two months until the Cambrai tank attack, November 20th 1917, was about the best time I ever had in the front line in France. There was no shelling, trench mortar, or machine gun fire because our front line was about one and three quarter miles away from the German Hindenburg line. The fortified village of Moeuvres was straight in front, behind the first German trench system with Bourlon Wood on rising ground about one mile further back.

What a strange area – you went up to the front line over fields and farm tracks; in fact the reserve line in this section was in a sunken road with bivvies cut into the side of the road. Then just behind a small ridge was a communication trench of a few hundred yards and you were in the front line post. The front line was a series of posts each manned by about thirty men and connected by a trench some hundred yards long to the next post. From the front line you could sit on the top of the trench and look over the flat open country to Moevres and Bourlon Wood.

The notorious Hindenburg Line was a masterpiece of trench fortification and almost impregnable except for tanks. The

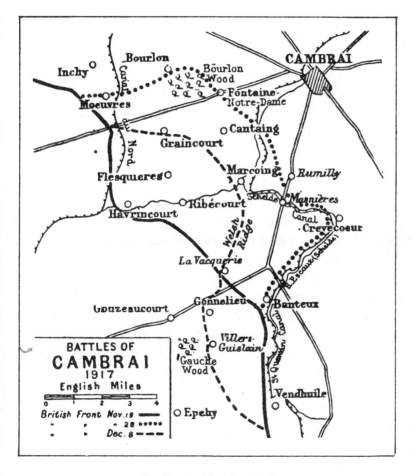

The Battle of Cambrai 1917

complete system was four to seven miles deep and consisted of two sets of trenches, one set being about three miles behind the other. Each set consisted of two trenches about half a mile apart. They had really formidable belts of barbed wire at least fifteen yards wide and five to six feet high. The Hindenburg system must have had acres and acres of barbed wire, and tanks were the only weapons which could penetrate this defence system. The Hindenburg trenches were so deep and wide that our tanks could not cross without bridging tackle. In September 1918 when we had a 32½ foot tank instead of the old 26 foot tank used in November 1917 the Hindenburg system was more easily broken through. There were tunnels, forty feet dugouts, concrete emplacements, in fact all the works.

Our trench systems were quite primitive in comparison, but we were usually attacking and did not need an impregnable trench system. We rarely had a deep dugout and we lived and slept in our narrow trenches with a bivvy cut into the side of the trench about two feet up, which latterly consisted of a curved piece of galvanised iron about seven feet long and small timber props which were large enough to allow you to sit up. This was the standard arrangement and if a shell pitched on top, you could be buried alive, which of course happened occasionally. The disadvantage of a deep dugout was that you never felt safe out of it, and you had a much more nervous time than when you had nothing but a trench. The only shelling on this section was counter-battery work with the noise of heavy shells droning overhead and we used to sit on top of the trench with some chaps taking pot shots at the occasional pheasant when it perched on the wire, but a ·303 bullet makes a horrible mess of a pheasant.

When dusk came it was a different story and patrols went out; heaven knows what for, as we never had a patrol fight with Fritz, though of course we sometimes heard him, and the patrol system heightened tension all round. The sentries never knew until the last moment whether it was our patrol returning or a German raiding party. With the Germans so far away it should have been a comparatively happy time but at night there was quite as much tenseness as when the Germans were three hundred yards away.

There was one particularly nasty job of holding an advance post on the Inchy road, manned only at night, about five hundred yards in front of our front line and out of sight over a slight ridge. The post consisted of two short slit trenches on each side of the road which ran ahead into the German line. A Lewis gun team and six other men went out at dusk and came back just before daylight which meant about twelve hours of standing in those damned holes and listening.

The Lewis gun N.C.O. was in charge, and it was one of the most unpleasant jobs I ever had. The Germans who knew all about this post occasionally raided it, and to safeguard the post from a raid men had to be posted about two hundred yards in front, one on each side of the road, and there they lay on the damp ground for one hour until relieved by the next two men whom I took out.

Apart from that, I went out in between relief times to see if they were still there. It was a really windy job and I can still remember the stealthy crouched crawl of those short journeys and the hoarse whisper of the night password to the two prone figures to assure them that I was not Fritz ready to jump on them. The knowledge that two sentries had been quietly captured two weeks before did not make this job any easier. The nearest we had to this type of incident was when one morning just before dawn there was some firing over the rise in front of us and our chaps came dashing back having been attacked by a German patrol. No one was captured and the N.C.O. in charge got the Military Medal; he deserved it for his covering action and quick exit with the boys.

This period from September to the middle of November with no casualties was a strange time, as there was no action and so little to do in the line. There was much time for thinking – for thinking about what life was all about and why we had got ourselves into this apparently senseless situation. After the traumatic experience of Passchendaele and my loss of faith in the teaching of the orthodox church I had plenty to think about. Doubts which the ordinary churchgoer often has, but which are often suppressed because one must have faith, returned with considerable force. The only thing that seemed to matter now was the truth as I saw it and that was hard to find. What would happen after the war – this war to end war was the question.

In the daytime before the night patrol action with the Germans over a mile away over the grass covered land and sitting on the parapet of our trench, there was a wonderfully peaceful atmosphere, almost too good to last and it didn't. One night about the second week in November we marched from our huts to the Bapaume-Cambrai road, repaired and widened it and most carefully camouflaged the alterations when we had finished.

This nightly period of hard work seemed ominous and sure enough we soon heard that a major attack on Cambrai was to be made. We were browned off and flabbergasted as a major attack in November seemed fantastic. Details were very hard to come by as secrecy was imperative. Some rumour trickled through about troops training with tanks and that was all. In the front line, every precaution was taken to prevent the Germans taking a prisoner. The advance post was abandoned and instead of posting sentries, half of each post stood-to all night.

The surprise attack was to be on November 20th and we were to move in and extend the breakthrough on November 21st. It was a strange business because behind the line there was little sign of any offensive activity.

I went down to Bapaume on the light railway on November 19th for extra Lewis gun equipment and was staggered to find no troops in the rear area, even our headquarter camp appeared empty. I mentioned this to our captain on returning and he seemed surprised but he said there was no need to talk about it. We knew later that after our attack and the very successful German counter-attack that three Divisons which should have been in reserve had been hurriedly sent to Italy to seal off the successful Austrian offensive against the Italians. This left the Cambrai offensive an absolute gamble.

The battle opened at dawn on November 20th and the first day of the attack was such a great success that church bells were rung in England. The surprise barrage and the hundreds of tanks employed led to the complete breakthrough of the formidable Hindenburg trench system. The massive barbed wire defences were so easily flattened that in one day an advance of over four miles was made – what an improvement over the months it took to advance the same distance in previous offensives.

We came into the battle on the second day and at dawn on November 21st we advanced over the flattened wire into the first Hindenburg trench; then down the dry Canal du Nord into the second Hindenburg trench, and then we moved along it northwards with our heavy machine-guns giving overhead fire as we approached the fortified village of Moevres, the village which was a mile and a half straight in front of our original line.

Our Company was supposed to be in reserve; in fact I think our battalion should have been in reserve but the action did not work out that way. Somewhere we took a wrong turning and, as the German trench dipped down into a flat sunken area about three hundred yards long on our side of Moevres which was then about six hundred yards away, we came under heavy machine-gun fire from the first Hindenburg line some three hundred yards to our rear. We started firing back, but there was nothing to see and a lot of precious ammunition was wasted but it had the right effect because quite a large crowd of Germans came running up the road (thereafter called Houndsditch by us). They ran up to us throwing off their helmets and packs and as they outnumbered us we would not let them get into the trench. I snatched a cap, grey cloth with a red band, worn underneath the helmet from one young frightened German which I still have; the name inside the cap is Schmidt.

One sickening incident occurred when one of our men, not in my platoon, quite near me shot and killed at close range one of the Germans running with his hands in the air and I heard him say, 'That's for my brother'. For his brother? It was just murder.

Some men went back with the prisoners and we moved out of the flat area up some steps cut in the bank, the steps being still in the wide Hindenburg trench, and there we stopped and we stayed in that position for the next few days. My Lewis gun team was at the end of the advancing line and there was no one else following. We were the last section of the last platoon of the 56th Division which was bombing along the Hindenburg Line to widen the base of the salient and which eventually reached a position known as Tadpole Copse.

We dug a fire step in the already wide trench, as with all captured trenches the existing fire step was now facing the wrong way for us and an emplacement for the Lewis gun had to be made. From our fire step we had a very poor field of fire because within less than a hundred yards the ground rose so that we could not see over the top, but from the top of the steps we had a full view of the fortified village of Moevres directly in front and of Bourlon Wood to the right.

Then I went off to find our captain, who was a new man, to tell him that my team was at the end of the line, there was no one following up, and that our south flank was unprotected. He seemed too emotionally charged to understand me (somewhere we had already taken the wrong turning), because directly I asked whether we should put out a patrol to try to contact other troops he misunderstood me, saying something to the effect that no man would move away from this position in this trench – we were going to hold it to the last man. The old heroic exhortation, and what a mess it was! We just stuck there for the rest of the day with the flank wide open. At the back of us was the impenetrable barbed wire barrier five feet high and yards deep so that in a counter attack we would be nicely trapped except there was an escape way down the steps into Houndsditch.

Just before dusk there was a lot of firing and bombing in front of the rise; I could not see what was going on. Then came men of the 109th Brigade 36th Ulster Division (I believe they were the Royal Irish Rifles) tumbling into our trench and shouting, 'What the bloody hell are you doing here – we captured Moevres and the

Germans have now got between us – why didn't you join up with us?'

They were furious. This tragic mistake has never been mentioned in any account which I have read of the battle. Moevres was a vital key point and was never retaken. Again there was the almost criminal lack of communication between the officers and men. When we started that morning, nothing specific of the previous day's advance had been passed on to the section leaders and privates. We knew that an amazing breakthrough had been made. As a section leader I had never been shown a map of the area, or given any indication of where we were supposed to go or what we were supposed to do that day.

My flank was now filled in by the retreating Ulster men and the Germans continued their attack very vigorously. Firing and bombing was going on all around quite indiscriminately but it was now dark and there was little to see so the Ulsters put a few men out on the slight ridge in front and almost immediately one man was killed from our own fire. The Lewis gun was not fired, for we had no field of fire and I was not going to run out of precious ammunition. After about an hour of bomb slinging and blind firing the Germans gave up.

There was a real panic the next morning when it was found how short we were of ammunition and parties had to go back down Houndsditch in daylight, running the gauntlet of some machine-gun fire from Moevres to get more supplies. These supplies were of particular importance as orders came that the Ulster Division and ourselves were to make a daylight attack to capture Moevres about a thousand yards up the road at 11 a.m.

This was going to be slaughter as the Germans were back in the houses with machine-guns trained on Houndsditch and the open three hundred yards wide flat level ground. The Ulster corporal next to me said that a daylight attack with that field of fire was just murder and I agreed. Then suddenly there was another change of plan, our orders were to stay put and only give overhead covering fire to the unfortunate Ulster Division. What a relief that was for us.

We were told that at zero hour a short barrage would be put over by Royal Horse Artillery batteries, who were about two miles back in the sunken road. They were our smallest field gun and fired only light thirteen pounder shells.

Zero hour approached. Sergeant Benson had just walked into my bay and had a talk with me about the covering fire I was to give, when the barrage started. I was walking with him and he was just one pace in front of me going round the corner when shells from our own artillery fell right on our trench. I flattened out in the bottom of the trench but Benson on the corner not a yard from me was hit by one of our shells and killed instantly. We put him on the fire step and covered him with pieces of sacking. There he lay for the next five days and nights until we took him out for burial. How strange that after fifty-eight years the detail is so clear that it might have been yesterday. The nights were clear and frosty and brilliant moonlight shone on that sacking covered body. I see it now exactly as then. I felt his loss quite a lot, he was a fine type and like me was one of the survivors from the Somme era.

As the barrage lifted we gave covering fire from the steps and watched the Ulsters trying to get near to the village. As anticipated, they were soon pinned down by murderous machine-gun fire. Our new Irish sub-lieutenant was watching with me when suddenly he dashed out on to the road and towards the village to drag back a wounded man. I told one of my team to find another officer to witness this. Our officer brought back a badly wounded man from some two hundred yards up the farm road. He was not hit and was off again to pull in another man but he was not allowed to make a third journey. I think it was worth a V.C., but he did not get that; he got the D.S.O.

Suddenly on the top of the ridge in front of us was a remarkable sight, an officer of the Ulsters was staggering about, obviously quite drunk, waving a revolver with the green Irish flag wrapped round him – heaven knows why he was not hit. The Germans must have seen him, he was a perfect target. Then we saw a man who turned out to be his batman and deserved a medal dash up to him, catch hold of the flag and drag him towards us. They flopped into the trench just to our left and then the batman came into our bay pulling the officer along on the other end of the Irish flag.

Just at that moment one of my team was relieving himself in the corner of the trench and I shall always remember the drunken officer saying 'Urine – urine – urine' as he passed through our firing bay. It was a tragedy but he had been through hell in the previous two days and this hopeless sacrifice attack in broad daylight must have been the last straw.

There was not one chance in a thousand of that attack succeeding with the paltry barrage of a battery of thirteen pounders but during the day we could see one group of Ulster men holding out in a ditch near the first of the village houses. At night the Germans continually sent up Very lights and the almost intact houses were clearly illuminated. To get some cover I dug what was known as a funk hole in the bottom of the trench into the parapet. These funk holes were very dangerous as with no support they could collapse and then one could be buried alive but many of us risked it to get some shelter from the elements – they were never used when shells were dropping around.

We were very short of food, but a little more food was found in the packs which had been thrown down in the road by the German prisoners we had taken. Their coffee tasted like ground-up potato peelings, and we did not like the sour tasting black bread but we ate it. I managed to get hold of a piece of fat bacon but it was no good as we had no cooking facilities but the Germans' full water bottles were very welcome. I am afraid we beat the Ulsters in looting these packs. On the left front there was a communication trench running diagonally into the German positions and the next morning while standing on the fire step looking out, a head appeared above the communication trench; it was a German N.C.O. with a peak cap, no helmet, blond with moustache, and we just stared at each other in astonishment for some seconds and then bobbed down. I told the captain and he put a bombing post in the trench. We stayed in this position until relieved on November 27th.

During the next few days we were not under direct infantry attack, only shell fire and machine-gun fire but we were under considerable strain waiting and waiting for the inevitable counter attack which was already being made on Bourlon Wood only about a mile away.

It was a very tense period as in our fire bay we should not see the Germans until within a hundred and fifty yards of us. On the right of Moevres the ground sloped up to Bourlon Wood, the battle line being bent almost at right angles, and we had a grandstand view of the intensive shelling and the attacks and German counter-attacks day after day. Although I had been in this type of fighting it was the first time I had seen what it looked like from a distance and I wondered how on earth anyone could survive such an inferno of shelling, let alone the machine-gun fire.

The bright moonlight nights were bitterly cold and one day we had a snow storm. We were of course dressed in battle order, that is no overcoat and no pack, just a haversack and for food we had what amounted to 'iron rations', that is dog biscuits, bully beef which was soon eaten, and water, for the six days from 21st November to 27th November. We had no hot food of any kind in this period and lived in the open trench.

On 28th November we were relieved by another Territorial battalion and I had a talk with the corporal who seemed in rather an emotional state. His section was completely browned off; they had been chosen as a shooting party to execute a soldier of his battalion who had been sentenced to death for cowardice and desertion after having been found missing and wandering about in the back area. They had shot him that morning. The corporal said the man had been out in France a long time and was most likely partly shell-shocked. This type of breakdown could happen to anyone. Days later on December 5th our Irish officer who had won the D.S.O. went beserk after a nasty shelling incident in which two men near him were blown to pieces by a shell.

How glad we were to go back and how much we wanted some food and warmth, but we only went back to our old front line about

146

a mile and a half and to the exact positions with the same bivvies as we had had in the previous month. We naturally thought we would go right back for rest but we heard afterwards that there were no troops behind us. What a situation with a major offensive on hand. The curse of it was that there was no extra food, still no bread and only damned dog biscuits.

During the day we heard that another battalion on our flank had had bread and hot food and we were all just as mad as hell. This led that night to what was nothing less than a mutiny when a party of Royal Engineers joined us and under their supervision we went out to commence making a communication trench from this old front line to the captured Hindenburg Line. It would of course take days to cover the mile and a half. The Company all started digging under the engineers' directions when after about an hour all our men downed tools and told the officer in charge of the food position.

The officers were astounded at the refusal to obey orders and appealed to us N.C.O.s to get the men working again, but we were all so hopping mad, eight days on biscuits, bully beef and water on a major offensive, freezing nights and without overcoats that we did nothing to persuade the troops to start work again. After a very long delay of over an hour they went through the motions and started work again.

The next day the fat was really in the fire, the fact that our battalion with its traditions, *esprit de corps* and all that, had refused to obey orders was unbelievable. There was the usual inquest but the whole affair was hushed up and by midday we got bread and hot soup! Someone was very much to blame for our treatment.

As I have mentioned before, the food question for the infantry in the front line was the cause of more discontent than almost any other factor. The rations were often so meagre that we always said that they were well scrounged on the way up to us until the front line men received a bare minimum. This Cambrai food situation was a disgrace. We could never understand why our cooks were allowed to stay back in the relatively comfortable camp at Lebuquière.

The next morning I heard that I would soon be going on leave, probably the next time out of the line and it certainly was about time after fourteen months. This long wait for leave for front line men was another major cause of discontent as it had been in the French Army with such dire results as it was a contributory factor in the great mutiny. Officers had much more frequent leave. It is unfortunate to hear of possible leave when you are in the middle of an offensive because at all costs you want to avoid becoming a casualty and the result is that you are in a state of continual wind up.

Then came the morning of November 30th when standing on the fire step just at dawn and looking at Moevres and the slopes of Bourlon Wood I saw a remarkable sight. There were groups of men and batteries of artillery pouring down the slopes beyond the wood. I called the officer and through the field glasses we could see that there was a big attack and it looked as though the Germans had broken through our positions. It was really an amazing sight, with a grand stand view of batteries of light guns being rushed down the slope and masses of men advancing. It was like a film scenario.

We all stood-to but at that time nothing much was happening in front of us and then about three hours later an attack started on our front and numbers of wounded men started coming down the road from the Hindenburg Line and across the open ground towards us. The attack on the 56th Division, the 47th Division and the 2nd Division took place just three hours after the main breakthrough on the southern salient but on our front it was contained; only the second Hindenburg Line was captured by the Germans, the first remaining in our hands. This was considered a magnificent action by these three Divisions and much praised.

We were not called upon, being in the reserve line, but about 2 p.m. we were served out with extra bombs and ammunition and left our reserve line completely empty to march hurriedly south and take part in a counter-attack to stop up the gap created by the German breakthrough. We marched a couple of miles and came under heavy shell fire at Boursies where we occupied a trench position and after about an hour we were told that the Guards and part of a tank division had returned and stopped the rot so we marched all the way back to our old positions. At dusk we relieved the troops in front in the Hindenburg Line.

Here we were, back again in the front line on November 30th after only two days in reserve, tired and worn out and wondering where the troops were who would usually have relieved us after an attack. The next two or three days were very tense and wearing as wire had to be put out to prevent the Germans walking straight into our trench, which was of course facing the wrong way for defence. All this time the shelling was very heavy on both sides. It was continual wind-up and there were many casualties.

On 5th December we were told that the 51st Highland Division was going to relieve us. What a day – the shelling was terrific. Our young Irish Lieutenant, who had won the D.S.O. a few days before, had visited the next Division on our right and had been mixed up with a direct hit on one of the fire bays which had killed three men; he had had a miraculous escape.

As he passed me, looking a bit wild eyed, he said to me, 'When you go out this evening will you take my British warm with you and leave it with the transport, there will be a G.S. wagon by the reserve line and you can dump the Lewis guns and my coat in that.' His coat would want some cleaning.

A few minutes later I thought I had better go along the trench to find the company dug out when there was some excitement – our officer had suddenly gone beserk; it was of course temporary severe shell shock but I understand that a few weeks later he was in England, getting his D.S.O.

About 4 p.m. somewhere on our left an S.O.S. rocket went up asking for artillery support – two greens and a red – because someone thought the Germans were launching an attack. Then the Germans must have thought we were launching an attack and up went their S.O.S. rockets. The usual thing happened and through a mistake we had two hours of most intensive shelling, both sides throwing everything at the P.B.I. of both sides. We all felt the effect on our nerves of these five days of heavy shelling and I was to go on leave if I lived through it.

The result was that our relief did not turn up until about 8 p.m. The wagon was where it was supposed to be but there had been casualties from the shelling, and there was no one with it and no mules. We did not feel like carting the four guns for three miles so I decided to dump them in the wagon and I was quite worried the next day when they did not arrive at the camp but eventually they turned up.

That was the end of the battle of Cambrai 1917; it lasted just over a fortnight, from November 20th to December 5th. It was however the most significant battle of the war as it showed that the tank, the land battleship forecast in 1903 by H.G. Wells was to be the vital offensive land weapon in the years to come. These early tanks, of which nearly four hundred were assembled for the Cambrai affair, were very primitive by present day standards. They could only travel at about four miles per hour and the male tank had two six pounder guns and the female tank six Lewis guns. The Hindenburg trenches were so wide that these twenty-six foot tanks had to carry a fascine consisting of bundles of brushwood which could be dropped into a trench and so prevent the tank being ditched.

After the first brilliant breakthrough, the hold-up on Flesquieres Ridge – a key position – considerably hampered the rapid advance which was so necessary. It was caused by one German gun which knocked out seven tanks, and this shows how one determined soldier may change the course of a battle. It was, however, the failure of the cavalry which did as much as anything else to seal the fate of this battle. A great gap had been made and for hours there was no sign of the cavalry and when they advanced four hours later the advance was much too cautious. As previously mentioned the cavalry did not fit into this war; on the 9th April at Vimy Ridge for some six or seven hours there was a gap which might have been exploited but the cavalry were held too far back. Cambrai was their last chance and they did not take it. As we had no reserves, the battle was to have been broken off after forty eight hours if it appeared to be a stalemate but the battle for Bourlon village and that dense square mile of Bourlon Wood went on for days.

It might have been a different story if the Passchendaele offensive had been stopped after the failure of 16th August. There might then have been sufficient reserves to ensure that Cambrai was taken on the second day of the offensive but as it was, the continued possession of this important railhead enabled the Germans to concentrate very quickly large forces for the counter-stroke on November 30th in which they took 9,000 prisoners and 150 guns and which was about the same number we took from them in the first days of the offensive. The total British losses in this battle of about 45,000 were not, however, on the same scale as the other offensives of 1917.

CHAPTER 10

Leave and Arras 1918

In a few days I was on leave after fourteen months in France, a disgracefully long time for anyone in the infantry, especially when the average life of an infantry man was about six months. When I arrived in London, I planned to call at the office, go to my old digs and the next day go home to Bristol. At the office there was a colleague also on leave. He had been the bright cheeky chappie of our section but what a change. He was quiet, preoccupied and very cynical. I think he had a feeling he would not survive and he did not. Some men seem to get that feeling, like the quiet one in my Lewis gun team.

At the digs, the governor, as we called him, gave me his best bedroom and what a strange feeling it was to sleep on a bed – it was the first night in a bed for fourteen months.

We had rather more than a few drinks in the corner pub and before I went off to sleep the governor came into my room and said, 'You are going to be all right – you will come through.'

He was rather strange that way, he liked to believe he had second sight. In any case it was rather reassuring if I could believe it. So far, the whole atmosphere in England seemed to be full of grouses and grumblings about shortages and rationing and most people I talked to seemed to be filled with an intense hatred of the Germans which we certainly did not feel in the front line.

While I did not directly talk anti-war, I made it quite clear that I felt that the whole set-up was useless and that even the winner of the war would gain nothing commensurate with the sacrifice.

My biggest clash was with my old headmaster when I went to see him. First of all he was very critical because I had not taken up a commission and he listed the boys of my form who had taken commissions. I told him that it had not been practicable but that I had papers for him to sign for my application for a commission in the Royal Flying Corps (I still have those papers – they were never put in). Then there was the recent Cambrai battle and although I was in it and was an eye witness he simply would not understand that the subsequent failure because of the lack of reserves was quite unavoidable. He seemed to think that something was wrong with the troops. He was a high-principled, well-meaning type, but British Empire to the core and when I said that I had never experienced anything unsporting from the Germans and that many of us felt that both the Germans and ourselves were the victims of a ghastly war machine which no one could stop, I know that his estimate of me dropped to zero.

Owing to this general atmosphere it was not a happy leave; there was very little money to spend as I had allotted all my civil pay, but that was not the whole trouble. There was a complete lack of communication and I simply could not get on the same wavelength with the civilians I met. It could have been my fault, but I simply could not agree with the propaganda hate stuff with which they had been brain-washed, particularly the macabre corpse factory lie that dead German soldiers were being boiled down for fat to be used as lubricants and soap.

People really believed it. The Harmsworth press went to work on it with great success. I was full up with retrospection and serious thinking and they were full up with talk of shortages and ration books. How disappointing after so much anticipation of a happy leave. With this attitude at home what was going to happen to the peace when it came? I had a foreboding that all the sacrifice of life on both sides would be in vain. This is truly not hindsight – I really felt that at the time – nothing had been learned and I was very depressed. What the hell were we fighting for?

Well, leave was soon over and early one morning I found myself at Folkestone ready for the return trip to France. The battalion had moved from the Cambrai front and was now in front of Arras with Battalion H.Q. at Roclincourt. This area was at the southern end of the notorious Vimy Ridge and about a mile up the road on the reverse side of the ridge was a deep railway cutting where advance Brigade H.Q. was situated and then still on the reverse slope the communication trenches started – Towy Alley and Tired Alley. How well named, because those damned trenches were about a mile and a half long and went down the slope of the ridge into the plain of Douai. The Red Line was just at the base of the ridge, the trench continued for about one mile to headquarter line known as the Naval Line and from there continued on for six or seven hundred yards to the front line which consisted of a series of large posts, Towy Post, Sugar Post etc. The sloping ridge with its uninterrupted field of fire was a marvellous defensive position as the enemy would have to cover about a mile of open ground between the H.Q. Line and the Red Line. This was where the Germans were beaten when they failed to break through in the big attack on Arras on March 28th 1918.

I had a fine welcome when I got back, the C.S.M. was very pleased to see me as he wanted someone experienced to deal with and instruct new Lewis gunners. Somehow I felt better than I had done for days. Fantastic one might say, but England had been so terribly depressing. There had been some changes, promotions and transfers but whether I would have been chosen for further N.C.O. promotion is questionable because I have always let it be known that I was not keen on further promotion and that I was prepared to stay in charge of the Lewis gun section.

Although we had not suffered heavily at the Cambrai battle a number of newcomers had arrived to bring us up to full strength. Some of them were from battalion headquarters in England. Sergeants from the English training squads who for the time being were privates until they had gained battle experience. It was strange to see the senior middle-aged sergeant who had trained me at Fovant (a grand chap), now a private and in the line for the first time under fire with no experience of the battle sounds which gave warning of immediate danger; that is the machine-gun range of notes or the noise of the shell which is not going to land near you.

I had quickly learned from old soldiers in my early days that to survive, no unnecessary risk should be taken and on this point I remember taking a working party from the camp up the line when the short cut was to go over the ridge and join the communication trench further up. This particular evening was very clear and I knew that we should provide a perfect silhouette on top of the ridge against the setting sun so I decided to go the safer longer way round and from one of the new lads I overhead the sotto voce comment 'windy bastard'. Luckily for me another party taking the short cut came in for a well placed salvo of whizzbangs. I heard there were no casualties, but didn't they run! When we got into the C.T. I said I had overheard the comment and I gave my lot a good telling off about the bloody fools who took unnecessary risks and had a short life. I told them about the devil-may-care lad who liked to show off in the Neuve Chapelle area by having a quick look over the top in daylight. He did it once too often and a sniper got a clean hit right through his head.

On this same theme I remember the Colonel dropping in on me in the line when I was on daylight sentry duty and peering through the trench periscope. He questioned me to see if I knew what I was doing and had a look through the periscope which as usual gave a pretty poor view of No Man's Land.

He then said, 'Has anyone been looking out over the top in this fire bay?'

'No Sir,' I replied, 'not as far as I know,' and he jumped on the fire step and had a quick but thorough look over the top. When he got down he said, 'Now don't you do that my lad – never take a look where you know someone else has looked, not today or even tomorrow.' That was back in November 1916 and I always remember the lesson.

It was soon time to go up the line again and the first six days were spent in H.Q. line. Here, in our sector we found an unfinished dugout. Steps went down about thirty feet and at the bottom was an area just big enough for the team. The snag was that there was only one entrance and if a 5.9 dropped on the entrance we could be buried alive. It was however a safe cosy bivvy although lack of ventilation made it smell very earthy. I put it to the team who, in spite of the risk decided to stay there.

After living underground and in trenches the smell of damp earth is often nostalgic even after many years later. In the make-up of some people there is a sense which triggers off the nostalgic flashback. For me smells are evocative of the past. The smell of privet on a hot day and I am back at the age of ten at the open air swimming pool with a privet hedge in Ashton Gate park, Bristol. I found that all battlefields had distinctive smells. The breastworks of the Flanders area had a musty dank smell; I suppose the rats helped. The chalk of the Arras battlefield had the dry tang of chalk, the trenches of Cambrai dug in clay smelled of rich earth while the smell of death and decay in the putrid swamps of Passchendaele was unforgettable. We lived in the earth, slept on it, and damp Autumn November nights can still be a reminder of the trenches, particularly so on 5th November when the acrid smell of powder with the pops and bangs is so like the desultory rifle fire which usually marked the evening after an attack.

We managed to scrounge some picks and shovels to take down into the hole and erected a marker on the other side of the trench to show the troops where to dig if the worst happened. The front line posts about six to seven hundred yards ahead were on the outskirts of the village of Gavrelle most of which was in No Man's Land.

It was obvious that the Germans would launch a major attack this year before the full weight of the American reinforcements became operative. For the first time we should be on the receiving end of a German attempt at a break through – a new experience. The Germans, having been on the defensive for so long had built themselves a marvellous defensive trench system like the Hindenburg Line which I have already described. Our trenches, with very few deep dugouts were primitive in comparison; therefore to hold the front line posts which an attack could so easily infiltrate seemed almost suicidal but the attempt had to be made and it was wiring, wiring, wiring, in order to strengthen the position.

The Germans knew this and their patrols round about the village gave us a lot of trouble. I remember one night going forward with a wiring party up a disused sap, where we almost stumbled on a waiting German patrol. We heard them moving the bolts of their rifles; we both knew we were there and waited until one or other of us got tired of waiting. Eventually the Germans went away and we were able to get on with the vital job of wiring which was much more important than a scrap with a patrol. This deserted village was a most unhealthy place for nightly patrol action.

At night we always put an advanced post in the village and early one morning just before dawn there was some excitement with shouting and shooting. Fritz had raided our post and captured two of our men, one of them was a friend of mine. An officer in the next post held by a Guards battalion heard our N.C.O. shout, 'Charge the bastards' and for that action and the kindly sentiment he was awarded the Military Medal.

One thing I have forgotten to mention is the attempt we made to keep reasonably clean but water was always short. It was a long way to bring water from behind the ridge and up Tired Alley, but the cooks were in H.Q. line and we got hot tea. To solve the water problem we used to save a little tea, then shave in it and try to wipe out the mess tin, but the next lot of tea always had a lovely soapy flavour – the price of cleanliness. Soon after that a non-lather cream became available, and what a boon that was.

The routine of up and down the line went on and one thing that was noticeable was that from Tired Alley narrow saps were being made for heavy machine gun positions which were very carefully camouflaged. Also a skeleton trench was made in an intermediate position, only a few inches of soil being taken out. This was a decoy trench for German aeroplanes to photograph, and there was no cover if attacking troops captured it. All this was very ominous and the question was, who would be in those front line posts at zero hour on the morning of the attack.

It was vital to hold Vimy Ridge, which was the key to Arras and the contour of the ground gave the Machine Gun Corps a first class defensive position. The history of the German atack south of Arras on the Fifth Army on March 21st and the subsequent breakthrough which lost us all the old Somme battlefields is well known. The northern flank of the German atack, however, failed to clear the way to Arras so the Germans were obliged to make a frontal attack on Vimy Ridge which they planned to take the first day on March 28th and on the next day to be in Arras. We went back to the front line on 26th March and it was clear that the attack was imminent and that we were going to be unlucky. The bombardment on the 26th and 27th March was frightening, and the communication trenches were very heavily battered and pretty well flattened. The tension was terrific – to be killed, wounded, or captured was almost a certainty but which would it be? For the first time we were going to be on the defensive against a major attack and it was even worse than going over the top.

I remember seeing an officer flat on his face near the H.Q. line almost unable to move. He was a medical officer, the first time up and he had never been in the line before. What an experience for the poor chap – a bombardment of that severity with no preliminary experience of shell fire. I showed him the way to the H.Q. dugout. Then I had the biggest stroke of luck ever – I was not to be in the front line post when the Germans attacked on March 28th. Our gas N.C.O. had himself become a gas casualty and his job was far and away the best of any – the really posh job in the Company. The gas N.C.O. was always attached to Company H.Q. and usually was with the Company Sergeant Major, who had selected me for a course of gas instruction to take over the vacancy.

So, at the critical moment with the German attack imminent, I was ordered to leave for instruction at the gas school which was over thirty miles back in the rear area at Doullens. I went back by train and we had some excitement when a German plane tried to bomb the train but he missed. When we arrived at Doullens I found that in the disorganisation of the breakthrough on the Fifth Army front, the school had been temporarily closed so I returned the following day to battalion H.Q. at Roclincourt.

The news was that on March 28th at 3.30 a.m. the Germans put down a heavy barrage of high explosive and gas shells and this went on for hours until the German attack at 7.15 a.m. The front line posts were obliterated, the trenches blotted out and the London Rifle Brigade was almost annihilated. Only 8 officers and 60 other ranks survived from a total of 23 officers and 564 other ranks. That was a desperate loss – the old battalion was finished. My poor old Company – very few escaped but a number of them became prisoners including our Company Sergeant Major who had been out much too long, and in the final reckoning on the day after the battle the Company totalled only about six men.

When I met the only other surviving N.C.O. I remember him saying, 'Well I'm damned, you bloody well would survive.'

Yes, I suppose it is all luck whether one survives nearly two years in the infantry and I had all that luck. The bubonic plague scare at Bristol, Edwards who was shot next to me in the wiring party, the shell which blew up my haversack on the breastworks, the shell on top of Half Way House which wounded the Colonel a few yards from me and killed men farther away, the shell which nearly buried me when my team was knocked out at Passchendaele, the Glencorse Wood incident with the German behind a tree, the shell which killed Sergeant Benson a yard away from me at Cambrai, and now this. I had much more than my share of luck.

The attack on Arras was a complete failure for the Germans. They were completely beaten by the defensive position and the tenacity of the troops, particularly the Machine-Gun Corps. As a battle, it was a great victory for the Divisions involved – four Divisions against eleven German Divisions. The Germans advanced only about one thousand yards in the whole day's fighting. The heavy machine-guns in their camouflaged defensive positions with a clear field of fire put up a tremendous fight and wave after wave of Germans were shot down.

159

Our Colonel got some publicity in the newspapers viz – 'Gallant London Colonel fires 300 rounds at the attacking Germans.' He was promoted to Brigadier General a short time later, but only a few weeks after taking over his new command he was killed. This was very upsetting news for us survivors. He had been wounded seven or eight times and it seemed ironical that he should be killed when as a Brigadier he had the best chance yet of surviving. I expect he was up in front taking risks as usual.

We came back to Bienvillers behind Arras but it was very depressing with nearly all the old faces gone. Rest was usually a joyful period – living for the day – but there was little joy in this rest period. The remnants were gathered up to make one Company and in a few days up came the replacement troops, and what a mixture. There were north countrymen, instructors out for the first time, young lads just called up, and quite a number of old soldiers who had been out before, and they had their own N.C.O.s with them. I had a new Lewis gun team and in it was one man, a survivor from the old 26th platoon at Fovant, so he was another one who had come through so far. He did in fact take over my Lewis gun team later on in May when I was gassed but I heard that only a fortnight after that he was killed.

With the old battalion practically finished it continued to be very depressing and at that time were not so sure that it was a good idea to put the survivors into one company. There was a definite change in discipline as the former good understanding system did not work out. This was not because the new troops were inferior – they were a very good crowd, but they were not used to our old system and we had to have more of the orthodox army discipline. We had a fairly good rest period and then it was back to the line and this time it was almost the same area as a year before in spring 1917. We were in front of Beaurains with Neuville Vitasse and Guemappe as the front line.

My Lewis gun team was in a reserve position near a burnt out N.A.A.F.I. hut and at the point of an intersection with another trench. For some reason the Germans must have thought this was a busy communication area as we were constantly shelled night and day. At night it was merely as gas shell attack. These shells went off with the usual plop when they hit the ground and the area became saturated with gas which was particularly in evidence when the sun warmed up the ground the next day.

Gas was always invisible – only a smell showed its presence – we practically lived in our gas masks and I often went to sleep wearing mine. It was difficult to get some men to realise the danger of gas and they would often take off their gas masks against orders and so many of these men were just committing suicide since the full effects of being gassed often took weeks to develop. The gas was the usual mixture of mustard gas and phosgene. Mustard gas burns up the lungs and skin, but phosgene was a poison gas which affected the heart. Men were known to collapse and die if they did any physical exertion after a dose of phosgene, the intake of which could not easily be noticed. Mustard gas had a rather acid chemical smell and phosgene had a musty geranium like smell, but neither smell was particularly strong. The result of using this mixed gas was that all gas cases had to be treated seriously and were made stretcher cases even though the patient was capable of walking.

I went back to our new captain to tell him that unless we moved away from that intersection of trenches we should all become gas casualties, because although by continually wearing the gas mask lung damage can be avoided, mustard gas quickly saturates the clothing and after some days the skin turns red and blisters form which are very irritating but not fatal. The captain decided that we would have to stay at this point and sure enough the men started with gas symptoms, two of them had neglected to wear their gas masks during the morning when the invisible gas was rising up out of the warmed up ground. They started coughing and then the red rash on the chest and arm pits started and two of them went off to the new Medical Officer only to be sent back.

I developed a very irritating rash and went to see him but back I came also. This new doctor appeared to know very little about gas symptoms. After a few days my rash became worse, so again I went to the M.O. with three others of my team. There was another more experienced doctor at the battalion H.Q. and he was very cross when I told him that we had reported two days previously. I was told to get my belongings and without hurrying to go back slowly to the First Field Medical Station as soon as possible and without any over exertion. Actually I felt quite all right except for the irritating burns and trouble with my eyes and I knew that very little gas had got through into my lungs. At the First Field Station I was made a stretcher case – what luck, and soon I was off in an ambulance to the next Medical Station farther back.

When the doctor saw me still in my trench clothes he was quite cross and asked me why I hadn't changed my clothes at the last medical station. I said that no one had told me about the routine. It was the rule that all clothing must be changed as soon as possible as the gas in them would intensify the burns. I definitely had not been so instructed, which was lucky, as with more intensive burns I might make Blighty. The next day by train and ambulance I journeyed to the Fourth Field General Hospital at Etaples on the coast and was put into a marquee ward which was very comfortable. It was all like a dream – I could hardly believe it – after the trenches it was just like paradise.

There were a number of bad gas cases in this ward and one man died soon after I arrived. In the bed next to me was an American from Los Angeles and I am sure he was rather a bad case as he spoke hoarsely, coughed quite a lot, and also for the time being he was not being moved out of hospital. Despite his sore throat he wanted to keep talking and I heard quite a lot about the Los Angeles movie world, but his chief nostalgic talk was about the climate and the marvellous beaches and swimming. He admitted to me that he had been too free and easy about wearing his gas mask and I am afraid that was the usual regrettable cause of most of the bad and fatal gas casualties as we had excellent gas masks and it was just downright carelessness not to use them.

Cylinder gas, which I understand could be seen, was not now used, and the gas from gas shells could not be seen but one always knew when these were coming over because of the plop-like noise of the splitting shell. As I mentioned before the burns caused by gas seeping through the clothing were never fatal, only damned irritating and uncomfortable. Mustard gas burns started with a rash, took days to develop and blister, but the penetration was only skin deep. After the blistering the skin turns black and my body had large black patches which were there for months.

I have given this long explanation about gas because in the Second World War so much panic seemed to arise about its possible use. In my opinion, after the first surprise chlorine gas attacks from cylinders, gas became the most humane weapon used in the war, if there is such a thing as a humane weapon. Just compare it with high explosive shells and machine-gun bullets. Becoming a gas casualty with superficial burns saved the lives of countless soldiers and I am fairly certain it saved mine. I have already mentioned that my replacement was killed on his next time up the line.

It was a wonderful feeling to be in a clean bed with clean surroundings and with attractive nurses and sisters to look after me but now the big anxiety was, shall I get to England or just spend some weeks in convalescence at the base hospital, be retrained at the base and then pushed back up the line again. This was of course the fate of all lightly wounded men and so desperately disappointing for them. It was a case of so near and yet so far. How different was this general attitude from the lying propaganda stories of wounded men saying that they were sorry for being wounded as they wanted to be in at the end. After the best part of two years' front line fighting I had had enough; all I wanted was to get to England and out of the army as soon as possible.

The vital moment came the next morning when the Medical Officer, an old man with the rank of Major accompanied by his retinue, made his first and important examination. It was very thorough and I must admit that I looked rather bad, with extensive burns all over my chest and abdomen, but I knew that my lungs had been hardly affected and it was strange how difficult it seemed for·doctors at that time to be sure about phosgene poisoning.

Well, it happened – and the prized tab which signified that I was for England the next morning was attached to the chart at the bottom of my bed. I was not told by the doctor and it was my American friend who explained its significance. But at 3 p.m. that afternoon the bottom fell out of my world; a sister came along and, without a word, removed the tab. The American said that I wouldn't make it now as they probably had a full boat with more severe casualties.

When I asked him what I could do about it he said, 'Nothing, I have known this happen before' and it all depended on whether the Major gave me another examination. If he passed me by the next morning, that would probably be it. Until then I had been ravenously hungry because for days I had been on a light diet and being fairly fit I felt half starved, so much so that I had asked for second helpings which had been firmly refused. I wanted no second helpings that day, my desire to eat and sleep disappeared.

The next morning when the Major appeared in the ward I was really strung up, would he or wouldn't he – and without any exaggeration I thought it was going to be one of the vital moments in my life and I expect it was. However my luck was in – he glanced at me as he was about to pass my bed, looked at my chart and proceeded to give me another examination. Perhaps it was the power of mind over matter and wishful thinking for when my bandages came off the burns looked really beautiful with some nice new blisters – much more developed and severe than on the previous day and the Blighty tab went back.

Then it was goodbye and good luck to my American friend but I am afraid he was permanently damaged. Off I went by ambulance to the hospital ship at Boulogne where I was carried on board by German prisoners. I must say that all this stretcher business when I felt fairly fit made·me feel a bit of a fraud but regulations about gas cases were now always rigorously carried out. After that it was Dover, and the hospital train, and the first stop was at the Olympia station, Kensington. Even now we were not· told of our final destination and that was the big question.

Then we had a long long journey to Edinburgh where we arrived early next morning. Here something must be said about the adulation accorded to wounded men – the men in blue when they were convalescent, and in the First World War all wounded soldiers had the hero treatment. At every station – and this was 1918 – hospital trains were met by girls with chocolates and cigarettes for their heroes. There was nothing like that in the Second World War where more civilians were killed than soldiers.

I seem always to be talking about luck, but again my luck held for I was in the last ambulance from the train and by the time I arrived at Seafield War Hospital the medical wards were full and I was the one medical casualty to be put in a surgical ward; I was in fact the odd man out, and what a blessing it proved. For one thing life is quieter in the surgical ward as the nights are much less disturbed than in the medical ward where the patients are ill. The nurses and sisters in my ward were a very nice crowd and it was all very comfortable and cosy. The woman doctor was Japanese but I was never examined by her – all she used to say was that I ought to see the doctor in a medical ward. I was in bed only about six days when off came the bandages and I was up. I never saw a doctor in a medical ward, in fact I never saw any doctor during my time in hospital. The Japanese doctor never asked any questions and the sisters and nurses were only too pleased to have a fit handy man about the ward and they all joined in the conspiracy.

I was a forgotten man and very pleased about it, because walking wounded were continually leaving the hospital for convalescent homes and the longer I stayed in the hospital the longer my retraining would be delayed and with luck the war might be over before I was ordered back to France.

That was the general thinking and it worked out that way, for when months later the Australians took over the hospital and we were cleared out, I was not in the hospital records and it was a job to get me into circulation again as a British soldier. To get uniform and equipment for a man with no record proved quite a problem.

I thoroughly enjoyed the three months I spent in hospital, it was very hard work but very satisfying. There were no medical orderlies in the hospital and the ward staffs were fortunate to have me on hand for bed making, helping with the dressings, and going errands to the hospital shop, and sometimes to Edinburgh for the casualties in bed. I often managed to go into Edinburgh and many times sat reading in the Princes Street Gardens by the Scott Memorial. Another place often visited was Portobello, the sea front of which could be seen from the hospital windows.

The Scottish hospitality for wounded soldiers was almost overwhelming, and for those able to get out there were continual invitations to large tea parties and outings to the surrounding beauty spots, one of which was Rosslyn with its fine chapel inside which was the famous 'Prentice Pillar'. I simply had to refuse some of the tea parties as they were so numerous.

While in hospital I learned to play chess and in the ward played many games until midnight as the summer nights in Scotland never became really dark. To be able to play chess was necessary if one wished to join the chess parties of a Miss Melville Balfour who was a frequent visitor to the hospital and would send her carriage and coachman to convey a select party of four or five chess players to her fine house somewhere in Edinburgh. We dined in a fine oak panelled dining room and played chess with a number of retired Edinburgh people. It was all very nice and civilised.

Naturally in a hospital the rules about times of return were quite strict but I was given a lot of freedom by the night sisters – one of them was particularly helpful, when, if I was out too late she would arrange the bolster in my bed to make it seem occupied in case the matron made one of her infrequent visits. There was a golf course on one side of the hospital and there was a place where I could get over the wall.

There was another incident which clearly showed the war hero attitude. One Sunday when walking on the Portobello sea front with a man who had had numerous operations for a smashed up hand and arm, and always looked very pale and worn, we were stopped by a well dressed elderly woman who after a few words of sympathy pushed a one pound note into each of our pockets and was away before we could make any comment. With that largesse we took the tram to Port Seaton and had a good celebration. All good things have to end, I suppose, and the advent of the Australians was the factor which caused my departure, otherwise I might have seen the war out at Seafield.

I was posted to my battalion which was encamped at Blackdown not far from Aldershot. Nothing of any real interest happened to me here except during the last three weeks. For the overseas men it was just a period of training which gradually worked up to the standard where a full pack could be carried on a fifteen mile march. Then you were graded A.I and fit once more for the front line. No account was ever taken of the time one had served previously in the line. It might have been one week or my twenty months – once graded A.I it would be back to France, a most depressing outlook. The only bit of lighter shade was that the war was now one of movement; there would be no trench barrier with that three hundred yards of No Man's Land, so general morale would be much higher than the last time.

One item which broke the monotony of training was our strike-breaking exercise. The South Wales railwaymen decided to strike and this act of sabotage against the war effort was taken very seriously by Whitehall. The outcome was that the overseas portion of our battalion who in the main wore the gold wound stripe was ordered to proceed to Newport and stage a demonstration; so on a Sunday we were paraded and had quite a shock when we were served out with live ammunition. The situation was explained to us and we were lectured on the possibility of being ordered to fire if the necessity arose, and that such orders must be implicitly obeyed. Heavy stuff indeed – and off we went to detrain at Newport and pile arms in a main street while billets were found which for us was a school room.

Our arrival caused quite a sensation in the town as it was so unexpected but at least we provided entertainment when we

167

marched around the town, up and down the streets, with the band
playing and our wound stripes well in evidence. Well, this mild
intimidation succeeded – we never saw a railwayman to recognise
him and the next day the strike was over. Then we proudly
returned to Blackdown and if not actually with banners waving, we
had the satisfaction of knowing that we had not fired a single shot!

I have already mentioned the excitement in my last three weeks
at Blackdown and it happened as follows. One day, having just
finished a meal in the dining hall, I received a message that I must
report immediately to the Medical Officer. My first thought was
that this meant back to France again, particularly as I had already
been passed as A.I for overseas service some weeks before and it
was a very depressed A.I soldier who slowly wended his way to the
M.O. but it was far from that, it was for my 'ticket' – my discharge
from the army! What a surprise and what a relief – it was
unbelievable. All this was due to the fact that I had been employed
at the Ministry of Labour and they had applied specially for my
release in order to join the staff which would deal with the
allocation to industry of men released from the Forces.

This was, of course, tremendous news, not only for me but for
everyone, as the end of the war must be in sight and the news that
an A.I man was being discharged to help with demobilisation soon
spread all round the camp and beyond. There had been no hint to
us of such an immediate end of the war and this news was
dynamite. Officers stopped me, in fact everybody stopped me to ask
about it, and I had a hectic week or two in the canteen, being rarely
allowed to pay for a drink. However in spite of it all I managed to
keep sober. The fact was that I intensely disliked getting really
drunk as I got such a terrible hangover.

At last the time came for leaving and about 6 a.m. on 11th
November 1918 to the chorus of 'lucky bastard' from my envious
hut mates I left Blackdown to entrain for Aldershot and my
discharge. All was quiet when I left camp and also in Aldershot
when I arrived. I went to the discharge centre and first of all saw a
doctor who said that all men for discharge had to go before a

medical board. I told him I was A.I but he said there was no other method of discharge. He questioned me about my army career, and when I said I had been gassed he said that I should tell the board just that. I did, and I was awarded a small disability pension (ten per cent I think) for 'having suffered impairment during military service'. My impairment was certainly not physical but had they known of my cynical outlook on the war they might have made it mental. I was just putting on some civilian trousers, in fact to use army parlance I was almost caught with my trousers down, when suddenly there was a noise like gunfire. I quickly buttoned up my trousers and rushed out to find that everyone was shouting that the war was over.

Well, here was I, exactly on the 11th hour of the 11th day of November, a civilian again.

Then it was full speed for the train to London. It was not a fast train and what a journey! As we passed one camp there were huts ablaze; the Australians were having a real Australian celebration and at the next station a large crowd of them raided the train. A number of them were properly lit up and it was lucky that we were not in a corridor train or some of us might have finished on the railway line and I understand that one or two rode up to London on the footplate of the engine. At last that was it – *la guerre finie* – and I went back to my old digs in Kensington where I was told the next morning that I finished up Armistice Day dancing on the counter of the corner pub. I simply do not remember – I must have passed out, but it was only the third time in my life, (1) the Neuve Chapelle wiring party, (2) the 1917 Company Christmas dinner, and now (3) 11th November 1918. Not a bad record so far.

So this was the end of army life for me which commenced with an unusual enlistment episode and finished with a dramatic A.I discharge precisely at the 11th hour on the 11th day. I was one of the lucky survivors of the P.B.I., but what about the millions who did not survive? The following table of the main battles in 1916/1917 shows clearly the cost in human lives of the policy of attrition:

Year	Place	Total Penetration	Attacker	Approximate Casualties
1916	Verdun	5 miles	German	348,000 French 328,000 German
1916	Somme	4 miles	British	500,000 British (20,000 killed) July 1st 450,000 German 204,000 French
1917	Arras	4 miles	British	190,000 British
1917	Aisne	3 miles	French	150,000 French
1917	Ypres	4½ miles	British	600,000 British 178,000 German

The above table shows that the Allied casualties in this period of about nineteen months were approximately one and three quarter million for a penetration of three to five miles on fronts which totalled only some forty miles.

The figures are appalling but I realise that the horrors written about that war and cold statistics cannot by themselves have much impact on the younger generation. For them this long ago war is just history, but is it not possible for them to sense something of the waste, degradation, and the pity of war through the poems of the war poets and this type of narrative which tells the experienced truth, not so much about battles but about the emotions felt by the soldier in battle? Truths untold which are so often buried deep even by survivors, for one must not admit to being frightened; must not admit how it satisfies the ego to make light of danger when danger is passed and then adopt the stiff upper lip attitude; and must not admit that after the first ordeal of exposure to heavy shelling and machine-gun fire, one had had enough and wanted no more of it. The hawks will have little sympathy for this attitude but look at the disastrous record of their policies. If something of the futility of war does not strike a responsive chord in the youth of this generation these few chapters about the P.B.I. will have been to no purpose.

With the end of the war the question was the peace – the peace which would create a new world without war, for which millions had died. In the atmosphere of hate which had not diminished since my leave in England I felt very pessimistic. In the months of that eternal wrangling in Paris between the patriots of each victorious nation, I often wished that a paraphrase of part of Lincoln's Gettysburg speech had been placed daily in front of them:

> That we here highly resolve that these dead shall not have died in vain – that these nations under God shall have a new birth of freedom – and that government of the people by the people for the people shall not perish from the earth.

It was a vain hope – they died in vain. I remember the many arguments I had with friends and particularly older people about the paramount need for reconciliation. It was a duty to the dead of all nations. We were all to blame, but in dealing with defeated Germany the politicians of the various countries were determined in the words of Geddes, our Minister of Reconstruction, to 'get everything out of her that you can squeeze out of a lemon and a bit more'. No heed was taken of Nurse Cavell's words 'Patriotism is not enough, I must have no hatred or bitterness towards anyone', nor of Wilfred Owen's line 'They who love the greater love lay down their life; they do not hate'.

The greater love was very far from the thoughts of those delegates filled with patriotic zeal and so the Versailles Peace Treaty – a treaty of merciless severity was imposed on the vanquished, and the blockade of Germany was also mercilessly maintained so that thousands and thousands of Germans died from malnutrition. Civilians who had little to do with the making of war – just human beings who had been unfortunate enough to have been born in Germany. Why cannot our children be taught that the seeds of the Second World War were well and truly sown in that Treaty and although there was a twenty year period of germination the bloody harvest of the Second World War was inevitable? Why not explain that the vengeful Treaty of Versailles provided very fertile ground for the madman Hitler to brainwash the German people with his warlike Nazi philosophy and that if only reconciliation had been the theme the Second World War might not have happened?

Have we learned anything from our wars or does each generation start off with the same wrong values of life? Wrong values which some day will have to be paid for with useless sacrifices? Can the younger generation undermine and eventually destroy the false idols of power and bellicose patriotism which older generations still enshrine? Will the epilogue addressed primarily to the grandchildren of my generation have any impact on them and stir up discussions about the present state of our society and the danger of the Third World War? I hope so because some day, somehow, humanity must find a way to peace and true values.

We are too complacent. We are all sitting on a powder keg and if only some of the complacency can be disturbed even a little by this narrative I feel the writing of it has been worth while.

Epilogue

This factual unexaggerated story of man's inhumanity to man which happened over half a century ago is dedicated to you, the grandchildren of my generation, as any hope of a better future – a future without wars – must lie with you, the youth of to-day. The old are too old, and as for the middle-aged, your parents, so many are involved with family responsibilities and the pressures of modern competitive living that generally they must strive to retain the status quo and shun large adventurous changes in their mode of life, but you young people have the time, opportunity, and capacity for creating a better society.

In the preceding pages I have tried to show something of the pity of war – the hollowness of the glory of dying for King and Country – the hollowness of pseudo patriotism so often fostered by vested interests which sets man against man in an orgy of blind killing. For those who have to do the close range killing there is no glory, no worthwhile heroism or self sacrifice in the decadent soul destroying exercise of war. I could write and go on writing about the horrors of that long ago war and those of the Second World War but such writing can have little effect on the younger generation as experience can rarely be transmitted.

However the story about life and death in the ranks of the P.B.I. is not so vital or important as the beliefs and opinions expressed in this epilogue. I know that it has all been said before – much better than I can say it, but possibly not in this urgent context. Only just in time the nations of the world have been awakened to the appalling man made build up of pollution in our air, rivers, lakes, seas and land, so perhaps just in time we can be awakened to the appalling build up of armaments for the Third World War. War in August 1914 came unexpectedly out of the blue – the next war can come in a flash and it may be the final flash. Do not believe the armament mongers whose propaganda is that the more armaments we have the better the chance of peace. It never has been so and never will be so.

One indisputable fact is that the economic rock base of our democratic civilisation is the manufacture of arms. Never before in the history of the world, in time of peace, has so much wealth been expended in making weapons to kill our own kind. It is now, as it always has been, the most profitable business in the world. This country this year is spending some five thousand millions on defence and we have a flourishing export business in murder weapons. We supply arms to almost anyone in the world and our conscience is clear because all these arms are for defence – the old lie which no one really believes. If you protest against this traffic you will be reminded that it is necessary for our economy otherwise there will be much more unemployment. The manufacture of arms was Hitler's solution for the German unemployment problem. So make no mistake, under a way of life where the chief aim is material gain there is not the remotest chance of large scale disarmament – there is too much profit in it. All the present style peace propaganda, Aldermaston marches, and the prayers of the Church appear to be just waste of time. The powerful agents of international armament manufacturers long ago named by Beverley Nichols as 'The Bloody International Limited' would wreck any serious attempt at disarmament in the same way as the agents of American Steel Corporations helped to wreck the post war Henderson Geneva Conference.

Then let us consider the position of the Church; it should be the greatest and most effective pacifist institution but in time of war almost all national churches in each country pray for victory – they all condone national wars. Again, our churches, abbeys and

174

cathedrals are littered with the emblems of war, defaced with plaques to the memory of individual officers of our fighting forces and reminders of campaigns in India, Egypt, South Africa etc. The tomb of the Unknown Soldier in Westminster Abbey is inscribed with the words 'FOR GOD · FOR KING · FOR COUNTRY'. The buckle of the belt of every German soldier in this war had blazoned on it 'GOTT MIT UNS' (God with us). Was God a partner in the holocaust? Do not these slogans verge on blasphemy? Look again at the Regimental Colours reverently hung in the churches as though they were holy relics. Is there any need to ask what the judgment of Christ would be about such sacrilege; what on earth or in heaven has the glorification of war to do with God? I would remove the lot – their place is not in the house of God but in a war museum.

That there is little protest about this and similar attitudes to armaments and war shows how effectively we have been conditioned from our earliest years to accept things as they are, but there comes a time and that time is now when traditional attitudes must be questioned and old idols destroyed. We are living in a sick society with corruption in high places, with a monetary crisis, and with crime and violence on an ever increasing scale. There must be some drastic changes in our way of life but I must warn you young people that if to minimise the risk of the Third World War you talk about changes you may be labelled as a revolutionary.

The report of the Royal Commission which makes the periodical research concerning the distribution of income and wealth of this country states that more than one quarter of all personal wealth is owned by the richest 1 per cent of the population; about half of all the wealth is owned by the richest 5 per cent and two-thirds by the richest 10 per cent. These people in power, that small minority who wish to maintain the status quo, will do everything they can to stave off any reforms which might threaten their privileged position.

Perhaps a gloomy picture but not all gloom as we are living in one of the greatest periods of change in history, but in the face of opposition to change how can a more ethical and peace loving society emerge?

The doctrine about the brotherhood of man and peace has been the recurring theme of idealists and world religions for thousands of years and you can say possibly with some cynicism just look at the state of the world to-day – split as never before into warring and potentially warring societies, so why waste time talking about pacifism and better ways of living. Man is a fighter and through the evolutionary climb through a hundred thousand and more years he has had to fight for survival. This fighting instinct is ingrained and you will say that all the goody goody preaching by idealists cannot alter that. The ethics of the Sermon on the Mount are beautiful and uplifting on Sunday but in our modern competitive society for the rest of the week they are quite impracticable, so forget them – just keep them for Sunday. That very generally is the status quo position and it must be admitted that the evolutionary climb up the tree of life has in fact resulted in the survival of the fittest and could be called a law of nature. But, and this is a very big but, we are at this moment in this constantly changing process of evolution at the end of an era – the end of an era running back some six thousand years. This is a period of great change – a period of change with an almost frightening acceleration. The technological revolution has burst upon us; the machine is taking so much of the sweat out of labour that we could now begin to use our evolutionary drive in much more creative ways and develop a new way of living without the present greedy acquisitive rat race. Galbraith, the well known economist, has said, 'It is not the increase of consumer goods that counts but the use of and the quality of life.'

The way is now opening up for the world to become truly ours by co-operating with nature and our fellow men rather than fighting them. By the end of the century as more and more machines and computers take over the menial repetitive side of our work the working week may even be reduced to two or three days and with a higher standard of living. This must mean a revolutionary change in our economic system including far reaching adjustments in our style of work and leisure.

Surely the hope for mankind must lie in this new era where there should be less aggression, more caring and in this situation the ideal of 'do unto others' should become more possible.

There are many books to-day which provide stimulating reading on a more ideal way of living. They provide a fertile ground for freedom of thought without imprisonment in orthodoxy. The optimistic writings of Teilhard de Chardin *The Phenomenon of Man* and *The Future of Man* and *The Perennial Philosophy* by Aldous Huxley, *This Year of Grace* and *From Darkness to Light* by Victor Gollancz, also Albert Schweitzer's *Reverence for Life*, and the numerous writings of the philosopher Dr. Alan Watts are some such books. The ethics of the Sermon on the Mount are contained in most world religions and the hope must be that some day these ideals will be given more than lip service.

I am reminded that in the Christian teaching there are two concepts which should have a great impact; 'The Kingdom of God is within you', and that we are all 'Sons of God'; for the Vedantist this is expressed as *'Tat Swam Asi'* – 'That Art Thou'. These imply that there is a spark of the divine in everyone. Can any man have the authority to order the elimination of that spark?

As Teilhard de Chardin asserts in his optimistic philosophy – Man is a miracle of evolution, the only thing in our creation that knows that it knows and a reflective being who can go on developing to reach heights yet undreamed of by us. Such a culmination can only be reached if values are sought which will enable the brotherhood of man to become a reality. You should therefore make your stand, make judgments, and sort out your position. A position where you can stand and be counted and not where you are just a 'don't knower'. Remember you are a unique personality, just as your finger prints are unique so you are and what you believe or disbelieve is for you to decide and you alone. This may be difficult if you have to line up in opposition to the views of your family or friends and you will have to analyse the opinions of the press, radio and television, the media as it is called, and not necessarily accept them. Apart from any of the 'isms' you surely must make a stand for peace and disarmament. You will be told by the pessimists that little can be done without changing human nature – do not believe it. I must reiterate that it is the type of society in which we live which does much to make us what we are. The new born baby has no inherent killer instinct but society can make him a killer; it made me one.

This story is entitled *Poor Bloody Infantry* and you may say that this discourse on material and spiritual values has strayed a long way from the subject, but my outlook on life was moulded at the climax of my life – the war, and if I had not been one of the P.B.I. perhaps none of this epilogue would have been written. It had been a shattering but rewarding experience which had forced upon me a heightened appreciation of true values. The war had been the crucible which had refined many of my ideas and the warning contained in Wordsworth's lines

> The World is too much with us; late and soon
> Getting and spending we lay waste our powers,
> Little we see in nature that is ours

had greater significance and would not now be forgotten. After so much death, every day of life became a bonus – every day was a new beginning and the appreciation of the miracle of life has not diminished as the years have gone by. There is an echo of that feeling in these emotive words I read somewhere:

> Only that day dawns to which we are awake. There is more day to dawn. The sun is but a morning star

It does not matter one little bit whether you believe in a particular religion, or whether you are a humanist or agnostic; what does matter above all else is whether you care. To care, you must be interested in everything around you; you must be responsive to the miracle of life – all life – not only your own. You must be in tune with the living world. For me it is the full circle when I remember as a very young boy the words of a text, which in the Victorian fashion of the day was hung over my bed and had on it just three words in large letters 'GOD IS LOVE'. It took me many years to see that is just what God is, in fact the only conception that some people including myself can have of God. I firmly believe that the increase of love, tolerance and justice are the only standards by which any worthwhile advance in the evolution of mankind can be measured.

This story has been rebellious, against war, against certain aspects of our present society, against certain aspects of orthodox religious teaching, and for me there can be no more suitable ending than the words of the American poet Kenneth Patchen:

> It's because we love that we are rebellious; it takes a great deal of love to give a damn one way or another what happens from now on; I still do.

Do you?

ERRATA

The paragraph on page 181 should read:

Wilfred Owen wrote, 'My subject is War, and the pity of War. The poetry is in the pity. All the poet can do today is to warn.' Forget the heroics and glory of war. The end is life unfulfilled - untimely death. I have tried to warn in this memoir, but Wilfred Owen in these three elegies, these three poems, does this with poignant realism.

The Pity of War

Three Poems by Wilfred Owen

Wilfred Owen wrote, 'My subject is War, and the pity of War. The poetry is in the pity. All the poet can do today is to war.' Forget the heroics and glory of war. The end is life unfulfilled – untimely death. I have tried to war in this memoir, but Wilfred Owen in these three elegies, these three poems, does this with poignant realism.

ANTHEM FOR DOOMED YOUTH

What passing-bells for these who die as cattle?
    Only the monstrous anger of the guns.
Only the stuttering rifles' rapid rattle
    Can patter out their hasty orisons.
No mockeries for them from prayers or bells,
    Nor any voice of mourning save the choirs. –
The shrill, demented choirs of wailing shells;
    And bugles calling for them from sad shires.

What candles may be held to speed them all?
    Not in the hands of boys, but in their eyes
    Shall shine the holy glimmers of good-byes.
The pallor of girls' brows shall be their pall;
Their flowers the tenderness of silent minds,
And each slow dusk a drawing-down of blinds.

DULCE ET DECORUM EST

Bent double, like old beggars under sacks,
Knock-kneed; coughing like hags, we cursed through sludge
Till on the haunting flares we turned our backs,
And towards our distant rest began to trudge.
Men marched asleep. Many had lost their boots,
But limped on, blood-shod. All went lame, all blind;
Drunk with fatigue; deaf even to the hoots
Of gas-shells dropping softly behind.

Gas! Gas! Quick, boys! – An ecstasy of fumbling,
Fitting the clumsy helmets just in time,
But someone still was yelling out and stumbling
And floundering like a man in fire or lime. –
Dim through the misty panes and thick green light,
As under a green sea, I saw him drowning.
In all my dreams before my helpless sight
He plunges at me, guttering, choking, drowning.

If in some smothering dreams, you too could pace
Behind the wagon that we flung him in,
And watch the white eyes writhing in his face,
His hanging face, like a devil's sick of sin;
If you could hear, at every jolt, the blood
Come gurgling from the froth-corrupted lungs,
Bitter as the cud
Of vile, incurable sores on innocent tongues, –
My friend, you would not tell with such high zest
To children ardent for some desperate glory,
The old Lie: Dulce et decorum est
Pro patria mori.

STRANGE MEETING

It seemed that out of the battle I escaped
Down some profound dull tunnel, long since scooped
Through granites which Titanic wars had groined.
Yet also there encumbered sleepers groaned,
Too fast in thought or death to be bestirred.
Then, as I probed them, one sprang up, and stared
With piteous recognition in fixed eyes,
Lifting distressful hands as if to bless.
And by his smile I knew that sullen hall,
By his dead smile I knew we stood in Hell.
With a thousand pains that vision's face was grained;
Yet no blood reached there from the upper ground,
And no guns thumped, or down the flues made moan.
'Strange friend,' I said, 'here is no cause to mourn.'
'None', said the other, 'save the undone years,
The hopelessness. Whatever hope is yours,
Was my life also; I went hunting wild
After the wildest beauty in the world,
Which lies not calm in eyes, or braided hair,
But mocks the steady running of the hour,
And if it grieves, grieves richlier than here.
For by my glee might many men have laughed,
And of my weeping something had been left,
Which must die now. I mean the truth untold,
The pity of war, the pity war distilled.
Now men will go content with what we spoiled.
Or, discontent, boil bloody, and be spilled.
They will be swift with swiftness of the tigress,
None will break ranks, though nations trek from progress.

Courage was mine, and I had mystery,
Wisdom was mine, and I had mastery;
To miss the march of this retreating world
Into vain citadels that are not walled.
Then, when much blood had clogged their chariot-wheels
I would go up and wash them from sweet wells,
Even with truths that lie too deep for taint.
I would have poured my spirit without stint
But not through wounds; not on the cess of war.
Foreheads of men have bled where no wounds were.
I am the enemy you killed, my friend.
I knew you in this death: for so you frowned
Yesterday through me as you jabbed and killed.
I parried; but my hands were loath and cold.
Let us sleep now ...'